A POLITICAL DIALOGUE

What it Means to be Human from the Local to the Global

Ray Newton

Also available in Kindle version on Amazon.

ISBN: 1491213361

ISBN-13: 978-1491213360

To the late Eric Kohn for the inspiration.

Contents of the eight tapes revealing what it is to be human!

PREFACE

The global economic, political and democratic systems are broken through lack of trust and must be repaired across the board. But how? Most personal issues are also social issues. These become political issues when decisions have to be taken because it is about how people fit into and contribute to the social and political structures. Otherwise we are in trouble and the neoliberal forces ranged against the necessary changes will dictate our future.

My interviewer was Eric Kohn who was a good friend of mine over many years and was an interesting intellectual with an inquiring mind which led him to think that a better world is needed. Some years ago we recorded Eric interviewing me and sending tapes about my political philosophy to his blind friend in the North-West Highlands who was interested in my plea for action, summed up in three words - Educate, Agitate, and Organise - arising out of our common concern to defend the Enlightenment values of reason, secularism and internationalism.

I am therefore indebted to Eric for starting this interview. However, his passion was music and he never exposed his great mind about politics outside his home - exactly the opposite of myself as a persistent doer rather than an armchair thinker! Unfortunately, Eric died peacefully in Edinburgh in 2011 but his memory rests for ever in my mind and I have completed the dialogue in his honour.

Many thanks,

Ray

newton@raypat.plus.com

TAPE ONE: ERIC INTERVIEWS RAY

Ray was usually early but today he was late. Then he made the lame excuse that he'd been delayed by some important mission or other. So Eric was pleasantly surprised at the knock on the door. It wasn't locked. "Come in. I'm in the lounge... If I had thought for a minute you were going to be late I wouldn't have had the kettle on - or the whisky bottle out of the cupboard."

My friend Ray was an elderly man, in his eighties I would say. I've also passed my four score years so we both go back a long way but who is interested in that? However, he came in with his usual alert expression that made me feel immediately that he was keen to talk but this time it was to listen, but not to me! I reached for the plastic bag in the corner cupboard, containing the tapes. Over the last three winters I had recorded the conversations we agreed to make for an old political friend now nearly blind and housebound in an isolated croft in the Highlands. "Kettle or bottle? Coffee or a wee dram?" I said as he entered the room and sat opposite me. My curiosity in his arrival this time was that, unusually, it was not about the flat; not about the garden and the weather, but about the tapes. Yes, we'd already had conversations about music, history, politics and the paradoxes of human nature. This time he was really serious! He wanted me to put the taped material into print to pass on to his family and friends. "I've called it *A Political Dialogue*," he said. "Strange title!" I remarked. "Well," said Ray, taking a deep breath, "the trust in politicians has gone so I've used dialogue to give it a much wider and deeper meaning of what politics should be about and not just the next election."

"Interesting," I said dryly and then pressed the play button. I'm always puzzled when I hear the sound of my own voice on tape, yet this was certainly Ray's!

***

Eric: Ray, before you start with comments on the political I'd like to ask you about your personal life. Some would say that you've lived long enough to acquire some wisdom. Instead, I have already read that you were named Raymond Newton after you were born into a working-class part of Southport on February 21st, 1927 "when there was a total eclipse of the sun and its path would not pass over the town for another seventy-two years when other shadows might eclipse your life." So why have you remarried at the age of 72?

Ray: Well, first of all I don't believe in old stone-age myths about eclipses but only for the fun of the thing. You could say that is why I was quickly motivated to move out of that town and saw the second eclipse from the Mull of Kintyre!

As regards the serious bit, I suppose that most people would find the marriage situation bizarre as the image everybody has of a wedding is a couple in their twenties with ambitions for a family and a long life together. Of course, many now live together anyway without getting married. This long-lived institution has been traditionally upheld in order to raise children or for inheritance and property rights, status and power, none of which applies to me! A wedding seems to accord less and less with contemporary needs and aspirations so it is therefore quite inadequate to answer that we love each other. Rather it is that we are committed to each other "for better or for worse" and that we wanted to make public what we had felt privately for some time, expressed very well by the former Bishop of Edinburgh, Richard Holloway, in his *Godless Morality*: "Marriage is about personal relationships, about emotional intimacy, about reciprocity."

Eric: Be that as maybe, I sense that there's more to it than that. I'm sure you'll agree that no longer should marriage be a means of 'ownership' by men in a patriarchal society. But inevitably, this has now led to different types of relationships, liberating for some, confusing to many but forcing everybody to rethink the wider implications.

Ray: Yes, and it seems to me that when people followed an unalterable way of doing things life was easier, but it also led to needless tensions and misery, sometimes hidden away as in Victorian times. Quite rightly, outworn traditions and stereotypes are now being questioned. However there is another side of the coin. Without an accepted structure communities as well as families can disintegrate. Young people especially become confused about what is morally justifiable and how to behave. We may forget that rights must be accompanied by responsibilities but the new pluralism forces us to think and respond to the actions of our fellow beings in a refreshingly new way. Indeed, life becomes more real, interesting and exciting if the new environment is generally felt to be acceptable and secure.We think as individuals but born as social animals.

Eric: You say "forces us to think" but surely it can also make people think in an anti-social way. Change may not be seen as change for the better and that's why there is opposition to immigration. I think you make a mistake at looking only at the social and not the individual.

Ray: Well, I'm trying to move from us as a bunch of individuals to the bigger picture, that of the historical and social implications. Surely we have to recognize that today is a product of the past. Nothing stays the same. We all carry unwanted baggage as well as a yearning for change but the disposal of the deadwood of tradition and unwanted legacies are also necessary in our party politics. That's why I think that the personal is social and the social is political. The logic follows that the personal is political. To expand this should we not, for example, give greater power and influence to the voluntary agencies of civil society to reflect the interests of individuals working at ground level in a participatory rather than a merely representative type of democratic politics?

Eric: That's a rhetorical question as far as I'm concerned. I notice that you have glided seamlessly from the personal to the social and then to the political and I'm sure there's more to politics than parties so let's move on to the vision thing. We all know that party politics is the art of the possible - about the here and now - but what about the deeper and longer term basis for thinking that way? The political rhetoric might have a pretence of being visionary but don't politicians like to be all things to all men in order to collect votes? At the same time aren't they merely advancing their own self-interest? With this in mind, do you think that the human condition is progressing and improving with every generation or is it on a downward spiral without hope of recovering? I'm thinking of the lifetime of the children now being born and not a policy for the next election!

Ray: My goodness! What a question? But let's not start by being cynical. Rather than take either of the two extremes of optimism and pessimism I consider the problem as a continuous spectrum, and different people begin the dialogue from different starting points on this spectrum depending on their personal situation.Young people are fortunately more optimistic than the old but one might sit between the two and call it realism!

Eric: Not at all! You sound as though only a middle-aged person is realistic. Optimism and pessimism might also be realistic appraisals of different situations people find themselves in.

Ray: O.K. I'll grant you that but let's get back to the bigger picture; in.

fact, to times past and present. Compare, for example, the optimism of Darwin's time with the twenty first century after the horrors of World War Two, Climate chaos, the international financial instability and the present commentators of doom and gloom. Consider the opinions we form from the way we relate personally as either winners or losers in our particular economic and social systems. The result is a particular mindset towards both individuals and humanity as a whole. Our attitude to the nature/nurture/free-will debate also colours our perception. Also, belief in divine intervention has been largely replaced by a scientific world view but we are still influenced by the Judaeo-Christian tradition of putting man on a pedestal looking down on a separate natural world beneath him which is there to be exploited. Our remarkable conquest of the planet has not, unfortunately, been accompanied by a similar advance in our wisdom and the present roller-coaster ride of consumerism is unsustainable. The ascent of man is now turning into the descent of humanity. That, I think, is the bigger picture and the challenge each one of us must now face.

Eric: This is a bit abstract. Can you be a bit more specific? For instance, what do you think of the idea of "progress" as we move from one generation to another?

Ray: The exponentially increasing wealth and productivity that we have seen during my lifetime has led people to believe in the inevitability of progress, of development, of a steady increase in their standard of living and of better health, recreational and transport facilities for all. The Marxist view went along with this perception but invoked the class struggle in order to achieve these advances for those working by hand and brain. They also talked of uneven development in both time and space, and of replacing the jungle warfare of capitalism with the more humane, people-centred socialism, based on a philosophy of not merely interpreting the world but of changing it. They held the view that man had evolved, developed social organisation and progressed in terms of individual self-fulfilment, in a series of dialectical jumps - simplified by the catch-phrase 'Two steps forward, one step back'. The ebb and flow of struggles within and between societies eventually resulted in a positive outcome.

Eric: So whatever we did as individuals Marxists believed that there was always a move to the better for mankind in general. In other words there is an ongoing moving forward and 'march of history'.

Ray: Not necessarily. Marxists rejected a 'spontaneous' view of progress but were sure of the advance of civilisation and the opportunity to better the whole of mankind. Now we are not so sure. A lot of marxism has now been outdated. Vast increases in industrial production have resulted in unacceptable levels of pollution, the depletion of non-renewable resources, soil erosion, global warming, refugees, violence and a downward spiral leading to ecological catastrophe in the twenty-first century. But this global political problem has also engaged my thoughts as an individual about where humanity is heading and hence where the younger generations are heading unless action is taken to remedy or ameliorate the situation.

Eric: If only life was so simple! I think you lecture too much and convince too few. Most people are just trying to get on with their lives. I'm sure they have their own ideas of progress depending on whether or not they feel better.

Ray: At this point I am only saying that progress is difficult both to define and to achieve. Now, at the beginning of the twenty-first century, I am not expressing the disappointments of an old man. My own life has been fulfilled beyond any of my earlier expectations despite disappointments and mistakes. I am simply astounded by the extreme depths and heights to which mankind has ventured and the amazing acceleration of changes both for the better and for the worse. The key point, it seems to me, is that we are now entering a period of great uncertainty. This is sad, perhaps, but it can also be interesting and exciting for those who want to try to get to grips with a new realisation of what the human condition actually entails and then to act accordingly.

Eric: Hey! Hold on! These are big sweeping indigestible generalisations - obviously after many decades of being a socialist and a humanist. Can we get down to earth? I'd like to go for the jugular and ask you, for instance, to fill in some details especially with reference, not to our own history, but to that of the Soviet Union? Its failure seems to have had a devastating effect on socialists everywhere and there seems to be loss of morale and confidence that we can change things for the better. Can you comment on this specific aspect?

Ray: Yes, as individuals we are a product of our social history and not merely of our genes and immediate environment. Our attitudes are framed accordingly. Those of us who thought that the capitalist system was the enemy of a fuller life looked for an alternative. For example, when Lenin wrote a pamphlet entitled "*Two Steps Forward; One Step Back.*" He was reflecting the marxist view that capitalism alienated man from his essential humanity. Marx inspired many people to think that it was in our grasp to change the world for the better and not just for a privileged minority, even though progress would be very difficult and uneven. Lenin then went on to campaign for a socialist revolution in the very impoverished state of Russia.

Eric: But the point is it failed, partly because of the view that the ends justified the means in a backward state of ignorant peasants. Then a ruthless leader, Stalin, was given the power previously held by the Czars and with the same disastrous consequences!

Ray: I agree but this is a question that cannot be answered with short sound-bites. You cannot say that without mentioning that the Soviet Union arose out of the destruction of World War I, then counter-revolution and the intervention of seventeen nations including Britain. Russia was isolated, threatened, invaded, laid waste in World War 2 with 40 million dead. It was then surrounded by over 100 American bases with nuclear weapons and the Dulles doctrine of "rolling back communism whatever the cost". Of course, anger, retribution, repression, power politics are not the answer. Stalinism was finally overcome but then Russia decided it had to respond to America's nuclear threat with their own weapons and to NATO with their own Warsaw Pact. Kruschev's new beginning came and went as paranoia led to a policy of secrecy and an arms race which bankrupted them, both economically and politically. In addition, there was no democratic tradition. Stalinism with the cult of the personality and top-down government led to political stagnation.

Eric: But what about the "command economy" that failed to give consumers what they wanted?

Ray: I think that the "command economy" might have been essential in the twenties as they had to pull themselves up by their own bootstraps from anarchy and devastation. But then the Soviet Union failed to give its people the incentives to react efficiently at the consumer level. Of course, there's a lot more that should be added to get, in retrospect, a better picture that the Western media has always failed to present. The most balanced account if you want to get a real understanding of the 20th century is probably Professor Hobsbawm's *The Age of Extremes* telling the whole story including many of the positive aspects of the Soviet regime and its countervailing influence against the continual attempts by America to expand market fundamentalism and dominate the rest of the world in its own narrow economic interests.

Eric: So this socialist experiment failed but not necessarily elsewhere as in Cuba, Vietnam or China. What interests me is Russia's ideological failure. Many academics admit that Marx's analysis of capitalism still stands, so what led to the distortion of his conclusions, not only by his opponents, but by various communist parties?

Ray: Due in part, I think, to the subsequent dogmatic interpretation of marxism. He correctly emphasises class conflict but this was narrowed down to exclude other identities such as gender and race and therefore there were class enemies to be eliminated. There was also the assumption that humans can free themselves from their animal instincts, perfect themselves and society and be masters of their own destiny without dealing with the inherent complexities of human societies and contradictions within man's nature. And remember that the word "communism" has been used and twisted to suit many causes and especially by ambitious individuals with enemies to defeat. We should really be talking about different forms of socialism and social democracy but take care! Many seem to be forgetting that capitalism is by no means a success except for a minority.

Eric: Even if we assume this to be so, history suggests that there are a multiple number of problems facing people at any one time and such is life that there always will be. What do you see as the main global problem today?

Ray: It seems to me that the most urgent problem today is the ever-increasing gap between the rich and the poor both locally and globally because of its effect on the community and indeed on the whole of society. Many wide-ranging differences exist between individuals but what we should highlight is the obcene wealth lying alongside extreme deprivation. The gross inequalities of an economic and social system continually favour the rich at the expense of the poor and their individual life chances.The resulting social injustices fuel crime, violence, migration, instability and wars that affect us all and I think that the answer to this must lie not in charity but in political action to change the status quo.

Eric: Let me add that if the world's richest 100 people shared their wealth over 2 billion would be out of poverty almost permanently but no-one except Bill Gates has volunteered to do anything about this.

Ray: Of course not! And we don't have to know all the answers before we make our voice heard to obtain a fairer and more just society. Lobbying politicians, letters to the press and demonstrations are some of the things that have been found effective as individuals. I remember the comic Marty Feldman saying "The pen is mightier than the sword - and is considerably easier to write with!" Better still is to join campaigning organisations and feel the progress that can be made in concert with others. After all, that is how society has been changed for the better in the past - if you study the history of our forefathers.

Eric: The tape was turned off. We looked at each other. I said I'd like a break and listen to some Bach and Ray looked out of the window to see if it was still raining. It wasn't but instead we went into the kitchen and talked about the workings of the new Combi boiler. We had to laugh over the new technology that always seemed to make us busier and life no easier.It needed some adjustment and he was always reluctant to admit defeat - but then resorted to the detailed maintenance manual. After a time I found his rather raucous Lancastrian accent a bit tiring and instead of starting the next tape I proposed we meet again on Monday morning. "Would ten be OK?" Ray asked. "You know you're really coming for the coffee," I replied and with a smile and a nod of his head he left. No, he wasn't late this time. I hadn't even made the coffee but we updated the weekend's news. I'd had trouble downloading my computer and Bill was here working away at it in the other room. I must admit that, busy as he is, Bill comes at the drop of a hat. Perhaps I pay him too much! Anyway, without waiting to finish our coffee we **switched the tape back on.**

Eric: So you've always been keen on political movements? As marching fodder or a dogsbody or what? Do you count yourself as a general, commissioned officer, sargeant-major or a foot soldier?

Ray: I've never been in the army or Salvation Army so I don't like being placed in that hierarchy. I've always participated in democratically organised movements for change. I'm not a specialist in any one aspect so that I rely on others to research the detail. I take up the position of an informed layman; a holistic, global and ecological view filtering the expertise of others through the prism of my own practical philosophy, gained from my experience in political movements over the last 65 years. Actually, my mind now focusses, in my waking hours, on nothing less than the future of humanity in this new century of ours. I won't see much of it but my grandchildren will. Future generations growing up in this brave, new and uncertain world will be faced with different situations and opportunities but they are being lulled into a false sense of security like lemmings enjoying the pasture as they move towards the cliff edge.

Eric: Why do you say this? Isn't it a bit of an exaggeration - an attitude that you are so critical of in the media?

Ray: I'm thinking of a way to express the urgency of the problem. Since the defeat of Soviet communism there is a view prevailing in the West that mankind is making rapid progress and will continue to do so except for minor blips, minor wars and accidents. We might be living more comfortably and indeed have reason to be excited by some of the changes and discoveries we are witnessing. For example, we have a new model of democracy in our Scottish parliament and the move to independence. There are more opportunities for cultural and leisure pursuits. The internet is making available democratic expression of opinion and certainly an explosion of information. We are also living longer but there is no better way to a crisis than ignoring the warning signals. It is my thesis that if we think globally and long term **all is not well for future generations.**

Eric: You're not one to see the bright side, are you? Do you remember that po-faced character Mrs. Mop in the Tommy Handley Show whose trade mark was "It's being so miserable that keeps me going?" Do you think that your world view is any more objective than others?

Ray: Thankfully more and more people are expressing their concern. It is true that it is extraordinarily difficult to get a balanced view of the global situation and its problems because people are motivated to exaggerate the issues one way or another in their own perceived interest.

Remember, the shareholders of BP perceive the world differently from the likes of myself! As I have said, we needn't be either pessimistic or optimistic. Rather we should attempt to be objective in our appraisal so that our vision isn't clouded by a view of the world only from our own successful and comfortable stance.

Eric: But if you were the Chief Executive of BP you would have to think like the present one. However, the important question I wanted to put is; to what extent is **mankind as a whole** moving forward and how much backwards?

Ray: The relatively few winners have a different opinion than the many losers. Worse than that, the winners all too often don't want to know; and, remember, these "winners" are our opinion-formers and decision-makers. Also many of the losers in the West are given to believe falsely that they too can be president or win the lottery! As the Romans discovered, those in power try to perpetuate their privileged positions by giving the people bread and circuses. Today's equivalent is a global diet of Macdonald's and dumbed down entertainment on television.

Eric: But surely the majority can't be wrong if they are given a choice?

Ray: More likely it's Hobson's choice but rather than engage in rhetoric let me try and clarify a few points. Blair wrote in 1999: "My vision for the 21st. century is of a popular politics reconciling themes which in the past have been wrongly regarded as antagonistic." I disagree. If we merely play to the gallery we may be popular but not necessarily right. Yes, there is a common humanity but all societies are pluralist with conflicts of interest and insoluble contradictions, like going through the day first as a pedestrian angry at the traffic, then as a motorist being annoyed at the cyclists or as a passenger in a bus held up by cars in the bus lane. Such aggravation is trivial and transient but think instead of the different identities and antagonisms of race, gender and class. So, yes, going back to your previous remark. I wouldn't be made Chief Executive of BP unless I was determined to maximise their profits in any way I can. That would be my aim and function. It's not a matter of being a good or bad man. Can we be all things to all men? I don't think so and I doubt whether the Blair Government, or any other, could have held to its promises under pressure from the real power brokers of society. Granted, this can be an oversimplification of what is usually called "the class struggle" but it is a situation that can be found all over the globe.

Eric: You sound rather negative. Why the pessimism? That's how the world works.

Ray: I'm trying to counter the apathy and ignorance on these questions so it may sound very negative. Elected politicians find that they have got to hide the truth and campaign for more of everything for everybody, knowing that the system favours only the top dogs and the devil takes the hindmost. But all is not lost. Human nature is not fixed. Our enlarged cerebral cortex allows us enormous flexibility. It can be remoulded despite the cliches that the poor will always be with us, or that there have *always* been wars and there *always* will be wars or that "plus ca change, plus c'est la meme chose".

As autonomous individuals and social beings we are not merely the product of our genes and our environment. Unlike animals we have the ability, if we wish to use it, to sublimate, bypass or counter our instinctive desires and environmental constraints. In other words we have sufficient freewill to choose, by exercising our power of reason. Therein lies the dilemma of this century. We have the potential but most people are switched on to "automatic" for most of the time.

Eric: It sounds to me that you want it both ways - most people can change but they don't want to!

Ray: Yes. I think we ought to be cautious about the speed at which people change as there are pressures on all of us. You all know the results of couples who try to change the other instead of themselves. Human drives to successfully procreate and survive were put in place during a million years of adaptation as hunter-gatherers in a hostile environment. It is fascinating to learn that mankind's remarkable expansion was mainly due to his selfishness, greed, sexual drive, and aggression. Now, however, these very characteristics are thwarting the core values of our civilised existence.

As Gavin Esler, an authority on America, says the U.S.A has "almost unlimited possibilities and hope for the future, coupled with levels of despair and wickedness unparalleled in any other industrialised country". In the West we have never had it so good but I suggest that we are deluding ourselves if we don't see that we are heading for a global financial and ecological crisis *(NB written in 2006 before the banking crisis)* as the free market is allowed to run riot. Worse still, most people view the present capitalist system as being the natural order of things, accompanied by the phrase "You can't change human nature". Unfortunately, the same people, by not attempting to reflect and change, often alienate themselves from the possibility of a self-determining and more self-fulfilling lifestyle.

Eric: Aren't most people in the developed world happy with their lot?

Ray: Studies show that there is increasing unhappiness. Even if they are content, which I doubt when I read the statistics of mental illness and the rising consumption of anti-depressants, we live off the cheap labour and misery of those in the so-called developing countries. Also those who smile aren't necessarily happy although smiling is very welcome. It seems to me that fundamentally the human condition is one of tragedy rather than ecstasy. Unlike the rest of the animal world people have the capacity to feel the suffering of others as well as themselves. We know of our eventual demise unlike the mouse addressed by Rabbie Burns: let me just look it up. Here it is.

Still thou are blest, compared wi' me!

The present only toucheth thee;

But och! I backward cast my e'e,

On prospects drear! An' forward,

Tho' I canna see, I guess an' fear!

But like those of a mouse, our genes have been programmed to make us seek short term pleasure for the survival of our species and not the long term happiness and self-fulfillment of sophisticated individuals. Does that answer your question?

Eric: Not really. I think you underestimate the number that think that people in general seek to promote the common good but selfish individuals get in the way

Ray: We would like to think that the greatest good will come to the greatest number as John Stuart Mill hoped for in the nineteenth century but are we not deluding ourselves? - that is, unless we realise that the powerful and wealthy want to perpetuate their privileged position. They can only do this by wanting us to shed our humanity and return to the jungle "red in tooth and claw" of the deregulated market forces that put them where they are? Spike Milligan once said that money can't buy you friends, but you get a much better class of enemy! Joking aside and for our own sanity, we find that it is essential to be positive, hopeful and to believe in our potential to improve ourselves. In addition, we have a defensive mechanism to remember the best and forget the worst. For example, we delight in putting on our rose-coloured spectacles as we look back at all our holiday pictures - all sunshine and smiles. The old days were far better - or were they? On the other hand look at the newspapers. It's bad news and sensationalism all the way. That's how they sell them and as Sir Bernard Ingham has related, after eleven years as Margaret Thatcher's press secretary, if reporters don't provide bad news they don't stay long in the job.

In sum, we have certain positive forces within us and some powerful negative forces impinging on us from the outside.

Eric: You know I've seen many poor people smiling and apparently happy and a surprising number of your obscenely rich sunk in gloom and despondency but, of course, I would rather be rich and miserable than poor and miserable. **Wouldn't you?**

Ray: Yes but there's a point below which people despair and a comfort level above which people are not happier but still strive for more, often at other people's expense. There's a story in the United States which publishes the top ten richest individuals every year. One of them became terribly depressed and spread his misery around until one day his wife pressed him for an answer. He had dropped down to 11th. place and his name was no longer on the leader board! So men (especially men) fight for status derived from wealth no matter the amount of the exploitation of others in the process.

Eric: So we have an apparent paradox. Can it be that we separate the personal from the social and political and not, as you have asserted, that "The Personal is Political"? Do we not dissociate our family from that of unknown others whose misfortunes we use in a cathartic sense? Surely, it's not all bad news?

Ray: No, but talking about bad news I'm reminded of the doctor approaching a patient in hospital saying, "I've got bad news and very bad news. Which do you want to hear first?" "Well," said the patient, "I'd better have the bad news first," to which the doctor replied, "I'm sorry to have to tell you that you've only one day left to live." "Oh," said the patient, "then what's the very bad news?" "Well, I should have told you yesterday!"

Yes, we seem to need a sense of humour about the most serious of things to keep our sanity. Perhaps this joke also reflects our habit of doing too little too late and I remember talking to my students 30 years ago about the effects of CO2 and climate change but it was impossible to get a letter in the press about such a ridiculous notion. Thank goodness the situation has changed and, at least, people are aware of it.

TAPE TWO: CAN WE CHANGE THE HUMAN CONDITION?

Eric: It was good to have a walk in the fresh air after listening to those tapes after a break of ten months… mind you, I think you're too serious about things. A video of the Two Ronnies wouldn't go amiss!

"Anyway, not this morning," contradicted Ray, "so I changed the subject but he had the insistence of changing the lighthearted comment into a planetary problem. So I called him from the kitchen as I brought in the coffee."

"Ray, I'm still smiling at that reference to the doctor saying "I should have told you yesterday! - but this is no laughing matter and I'm reminded of a presentation you made several years ago to the Humanist Association on Cultural Pessimism and asking you to put your answer on tape."

Eric hesitated as though he had doubts. "OK," one of his shortest replies. "Ray, when you're ready..." I wanted more than comments on the present global situation so I pressed the Play button for the tape *2.*

Ray: "Cultural pessimism arises with the conviction that the culture of a nation, a civilisation or of humanity itself is in an irreversible process of moral decline, intellectual decline and political decline. It seems to me, however, that the most important element is environmental decline because it is long term, requiring decisions now to pre-empt future problems. Human activity is radically altering the global ecological system, in the space of one generation what has taken hundreds of thousands of years to produce. Up to the last century living things have been able to adapt to changes in the environment only because the changes were relatively slow. Now these changes are too rapid for adaption to take place. Man is now an important ecological agent threatening his own survival.

Eric: Could you please be more specific, such as a list of the items to be considered?

Ray: The causes and effects have been well researched in the last forty years (esp. by Oliver Bennett in *Cultural Pessimism*). They include:-

1. pollution of thousands of synthetic chemicals, hormones, and waste products.

2. the destruction of the ozone layer by CFCs and aircraft vapour trails.

3. global warming by the greenhouse effects due to CO2, methane, and nitrous oxides in the atmosphere.

4. the loss of biodiversity - the mass extinction of plant and animal species.

5. the reduction of fish stocks due to overfishing.

6. the reduction of arable land through soil erosion and desertification..

7. the exponential increase in population.

But we will not all be equally affected. The effects will be felt first by the poorest on the planet but the rich, even if they lock themselves up in gated communities will be indirectly affected by the resulting mass misery, starvation, disease, migrations, violence, chaos and wars."

Eric: Ray, Stop there! My goodness, you **are** pessimistic! Are you saying nothing can be done about it?

Ray: No! I never say that! For each of these major problems there are possible corrective actions and there are pressure groups advocating these. However, there is procrastination by governments and the relevant international bodies in the implementation of the necessary measures because of vested interests demanding the maintainance of the status quo: witness the oil companies' claim that there is no conclusive evidence for climate change due to the burning of oil. "There are other causes" despite the conclusions of expert commissions on the subject. The complexities of the issues, the time lag between cause and effect and the selective use of individual studies are being used to delay decisions and the precautionary principles are being ignored altogether. This is not a recent problem. For example DDT was widely acclaimed after its first use in 1940 as a miracle pesticide and its developer Paul Muller was awarded the Nobel Prize for his efforts. In the 1960s fears about its safety were demonstrated conclusively but it took over ten years before its use was restricted. Similarly, CFCs, were found to be the main pollutant of the ozone layer, but it took a long time before an international agreement was reached to phase out their use.

Eric: Continue with what you told the audience that you wanted not merely to inform but to provoke them into questions and discussion.

Ray: Perhaps you are right. As a teacher I never stopped asking the students questions but I hope you agree that we have got to home in on one of the greatest problems facing us today?

Environmental pessimism arises from the sheer scale and accelerating pace of the threats to the environment as well as the unpredictabilty of events. There has also been resistance to the application of solutions now to problems that would only show themselves in the future, claiming that technological advances might then offer new solutions but there is a tipping point of no return. The scale of the problems and the apparent inability of mankind to apply solutions until too late to be effective have exacerbated the feeling of pessimism of those engaged in these fields.

Eric: You talk about feelings of pessimism but isn't this a rather vague and unscientific conclusion?

Ray: This, in addition to all the other aspects of cultural pessimism, makes for grim reading. Saving civilisation from itself is no mean task. The dilemma is that the potential of human beings to predict the emerging problems and how to counter them seems at variance with the lack of a collective will to take pre-emptive action.Unfortunately, this pessimistic conclusion becomes a self-fulfilling prophecy! The United States has already declared that nothing is going to stand in the way of its economic growth and power. Governments feel impotent to resist these aims. Hence the United States' rejection of the Kyoto Protocol, the World Criminal Court and its insistence in dominating international organisations of its own choosing enables it to have its own way to the detriment of the planet as a whole.

Eric: There have been instances in the past where pessimism was unwarranted and premature by nearly two hundred years like the conclusions of Malthus.

Ray: There are those who point to man's ingenuity to find technological and political solutions to problems, as in the past. Eric Hobsbawm, however, ends his great historical analysis of the 20th. century *The Age of Extremes,* 'We do not know where we are going. We only know that history has brought us to this point and why. However, one thing is plain. If humanity is to have a recognisable future, it cannot be by prolonging the past or the present. If we try to build the third millennium on that basis, we shall fail, and the price of failure, that is to say, the alternative to a changed society, is darkness."

Eric: It seems to me that the 64,000 dollar question is: "Can we change the human condition? Are we at the mercy of our evolved instincts? As a moral animal with free will can we transcend these? Is the present global economic system of market fundamentalism the only game in town, at Fukuyama's "end of history" or Thatcher and Blair's "There is no alternative" (TINA)?"

Ray: It is true that the barbaric history of the 20th. century has left people disillusioned about what it means to be human. John Gray in *Straw Dogs* echoes the despair of many academics about human capacities and ideas of social transformation. He limits our aspirations by *managing* rather than *overcoming* problems. Malik, however, suggests that the two most common visions of the future are either tragic or utopian and quotes Pinker "the existence of suffering and injustice presents us with an undeniable moral imperative. We don't know what we can achieve until we try, and the alternative of resigning ourselves to these evils as the way of the world, is unconscionable."

Eric: It has been said elsewhere that it is better to light a candle than curse the darkness but this is not derived from reasoned argument.

Ray: More inspirational is Gramsci's edict that the pessimism of the intellect can be overcome by the optimism of the will and it seems to me that Malik in his *Man, Beast and Zombie* gets closer to this truism with an historical and philosophical analysis of the human condition. He draws on sources from the science of human nature to the political realities of the world today; for example, after many chapters surveying the scientific "facts" including evolutionary biology and psychology, cognitive and social science, and a humanist approach to the way we think of the world, he says, "When socially we view humans more as objects than as subjects, more as victims than as agents, inevitably scientists will be encouraged to view humans in that way too. There is no incentive for science to investigate humans as subjects if, as a society, we do not consider our subjectivity, or "human spirit", to be particularly important."

He goes on to say that we are neither beasts (at the mercy of our animal nature) nor zombies (the passive result of nurture and environment etc.) but, to be brief, we **can** be potential agents in deciding our own future. Unfortunately, it seems to me that despite impressions to the contrary not many people strive to do this.The fatalism of Islam, Hinduism and religions in general is on the wane but minority "cults" have increased with dogmatic and sectarian declarations. Can Homo Sapiens use its power of reason before time runs out? I would recommend Malik's study because it's breadth is accompanied by a deep appreciation of how we have arrived at the present viewpoints from which we can derive hope rather than despair.

Eric: George Steiner wrote, "*The sum of my politics is to try and support whatever social order is capable of reducing, even marginally, the aggregate of hatred and of pain in the human circumstance.*"

This seems to me to be an intensely individual as well as social statement. Is this what you mean by the Personal is Political?

Ray: Yes, but I wouldn't dare put myself into his league. What I would like to indicate is that as one of the crowd, beavering away at grassroots level my life has been an interaction of both. From my personal problems my thinking spreads to the social and political. All my life I seem to have been questioning the views of the establishment and demonstrating against them. Some questions have been answered but many have not; instead they have provoked other questions. "Is socialism dead? Does man make history or does history make man? How much of us is the result of nature and how much of nurture? To what extent do our personal relationships and morality reflect those of society at large? How effective can we be as individuals in helping people to help themselves? Does each generation have to learn afresh by experience the problems and contradictions inherent in the human condition? Do we really know ourselves? and finally, how, in fact, do we live in harmony with ourselves and others?"

Eric: But these are merely open-ended questions. What matters surely are the varying answers that can be given?

Ray: In asking these questions we make assumptions and these have changed during the century in which I have had the privilege of living. They involve false dichotomies (e.g. nature v. nurture), changing attitudes (e.g. to morality), and much more. Can we take it for granted that we know what we mean by 'the personal'? Yes? - about myself as an autonomous individual; my private life and thoughts, my affairs, my needs, my opinions? For the sake of brevity let's assume that we agree on "the personal" rather than engage in a long philosophical discussion; although the 'self' is a puzzling reality worthy of it! We might also agree on what we mean by political as the term is commonly used to mean concerning public affairs and the power of decision-making by those in government over the governed - much more than the political parties within the system. However, the personal and the political are rarely seen as anything but a distant relationship and dealt with quite separately. For most people this may be the case. For me the two have always been inextricably linked and my mind switches easily from one to the other so I must be abnormal! This, then, is my 'problem' and why I put my pen to paper.

Eric: So what we are talking about is the tremendous variety of human behaviour and how we see the world differently even though there is a common humanity. Isn't our behaviour predetermined?

Ray: Perhaps I can repeat what I said at a presentation of this very subject At the risk of being simplistic there seem to be three factors contributing to our individual behaviour: - Firstly, the extent to which we are mainly a function of our genetic makeup derived from our successful adaptation during hundreds of thousands of years as hunter-gatherers. Secondly, the extent to which our behaviour and thinking is historically and culturally determined. Thirdly, the extent to which we have free-will, capable of over-riding the constraints of the first two.

Eric: So what is the proportion you ascribe to each?

Ray: This nature-nurture-freewill debate is not easily settled as there is a complex interaction between all three and difficult to disentangle but most importantly the emphasis of each ingredient in the "mix" has changed through time and place and some people exert more freewill than others!

Eric: Don't you think we can also ascribe something to a God of Creation?

Ray: Our ideas of what constitutes a human being used to be those of our religious leaders. Then came the period of the Enlightenment with a belief in the power of reason, the exponential growth of science and technology and an ability and desire to exploit the natural world to our advantage. We placed ourselves in a special position above and separate from the animal world and engaged in a sterile nature-nurture debate. Then came the discovery of DNA, the Human Genome Project and the expansion of behavioural genetics and evolutionary psychology. In consequence, we are beginning a new century witnessing a fundamental reassessment of what it means to be human.

Eric: I am given to understand that all living things start with their inherited DNA but humans are exceptional in their ability to learn and imagine different worlds and time-scales.

Ray: More than that. Kenan Malik argues that the retreat from human exceptionalism makes for both bad science and bad politics because the present attempt to understand humans in the same way as understanding the rest of nature ignores the essential quality of being human - our subjectivity. The very success of science, according to Malik, is hindering the understanding of ourselves. We possess, via our symbolic representation of the world, language, imagination, forethought and will. Uniquely we are both object and subject capable of shaping our own fate with purpose and agency. We are both inside and outside of us, both immanent and transcendent; not ascribing to the latter supernatural properties but transformative qualities, making our own history and not merely existing as victims of it.

Because Malik wants to explain and communicate complex ideas in an easily digestible form he takes 390 pages to reach a conclusion but this is a summary of it. The key problem is not that biology has invaded the human realm. It is rather that humans have abandoned it and we no longer think of ourselves as capable of determining our own future. It is this political retreat from a belief in human agency and from ideas of moral progress that has opened up a space for a return to a mechanistic view of Man.

Eric: That's a lot to take in and we are not all scientifically trained nor interested in trying to follow the so-called logic of everything and getting confused in the process.

Ray: Yes, humans need a refuge from science because our lives cannot be accounted for in purely scientific terms. Most people have come to distrust reason because of the indirection of human life. God used to act as a retreat from reason but since many no longer believe in God we must believe in the potential of the human mind.

Eric: Many equate materialism with a mechanical stance to biology rather than the Marxist dialectical materialism which is quite different. Where do you stand?

Ray: I agree completely with Malik who said that to challenge 'mechanism' which is a corruption of the scientific approach, we need not retreat from reason but to embrace it, for mysticism and mechanism are both irrational accounts of human nature and it would be inhuman to give up on the quest to understand humanness. What defines us then as human beings is our subjectivity, our capacity for conscious, rational dialogue and inquiry. This is what allows us to ask what it means to be human. It is also what allows us to answer it. Consciousness and rationality - these are not so much polar opposites as inseparable twins. Together, they shape our humanness and our capacity for both scientific knowledge and political conduct. If we ignore one or the other, in either science or politics, we ignore an essential quality of being human. That is why both politics and the human sciences seem so impoverished today. To restore a human quality both to science and to politics, we need to reconcile subjectivity and rationality, and we need the confidence to see ourselves not as beasts or as robots but as what we are: human beings.

Eric: So can we turn to another aspect and not just rely on one person's opinion. You seem to have been taken over by Malik...

Ray: Well, not just yet, if you don't mind Eric: For those who **are** following my line I'd like to address the key part of Malik's conclusion. In order to develop an understanding of the inherent contradiction posed by the object-subject dilemma, Malik devotes a lot of space to the history of ideas demonstrating that the context must be nothing less than the philosophical, political, economic and cultural aspects taken together. We can then move the debate forward on what science can and cannot tell us about human nature Eric, so what do other thinkers say?

The novelist Maggie Gee says that the question "What is it to be human?" is existential rather than factual and therefore Malik's answer is rhetorical. Susan Greenfield who is a world authority on the brain, sees mind and self as synonymous in the subject-object dilemma. Susan Blackmore, author of "The Meme Machine" says that "the self that is supposed to have free-will is just a story that forms part of a vast meme complex". Professor Kiernan Ryan states that "If self-consciousness, as Malik argues, is indeed the hallmark of the human being - the mainspring of our capacity for symbolic thought and thus our capacity to transform ourselves and the world - and as Iris Murdoch cogently argues - then art is the place where we can find that self-consciousness at its most articulate and profound. "Through music, painting, sculpture, dance, poetry, drama, film and fiction, humans have used their imagination and expressive powers to give voice and form to their thoughts and feelings, to represent their lives and their world to themselves in order to take stock of who they are, what they want, and where they think they are heading." We can then ask ourselves how probable it is that the world should be radically different from how it appears to us to be and there are also other sources I could quote.

Eric: Ok so where does this lead us?

Ray: It therefore seems to me that man's potential to overcome the constraints of his genetic and cultural heritage puts man in an exceptional category in the animal world but why not add that we may also be talking about exceptional individuals who are able to take advantage of that potential? One swallow does not make a summer. Could it be that people's views, for instance whether or not they are a pessimistic or optimistic, is coloured by their experience of people around them. A look at the global situation of billions trying merely to survive from day to day or those under stress from the pressures of competitive individualism, consumerism, insecurity and a dumbed-down media might see human beings with very little choice and free will to determine their future but I would hate to call them zombies or beasts. Also one might say that our struggle for a better life involves inherent contradictions and creative tensions between the nature-nurture-will trio, making it impossible to resolve what may be insoluble. Therefore, it is not surprising that Malik has stirred up criticism and I congratulate him on that.

Eric: It seems to me that we are stepping backwards. Let's move on.

Ray: I agree. The result is an increasingly narrow, self-centred view of humanness and an increasingly degraded one. I think that science is historically situated and a social activity. Yes, science certainly gives us access to a reality that exists independently of human beings . In this sense science is different from other forms of knowledge such as politics or literature but the scientific process does not stand apart from the culture it inhabits.

Eric: Now Ray, no one would mistake your profession but do you mind if I make my own comment whether or not anyone wants to hear them.

Eric: I have no formal training in science but I think that the entanglement of science and culture is particularly important to understand because there has always been an ambivalence in the way in which scientists have viewed human beings. Hasn't the development of a world view been in large part about the replacement of the idea of divine intervention as the means by which order is maintained in nature with the belief that nature proceeds according to its internal and immutable laws?

Ray: Yes, the arrival of the heliocentric universe displaced not just the planets, but Man too. With the Earth no longer at the centre of the universe, but merely one of the planets orbiting the sun, Man seemed to become more peripheral, an insignificant part in the order of things.

But let us move on by agreeing that scientists do not work with unambiguous facts. There is a social and political context in which they work and they make their arguments plausible to the rest of the scientific community. How do you see the future of mankind? Perhaps we can then remind ourselves that the growing confidence in human capacities made possible the drive to exploit nature for man's benefit. A mechanical approach broke up the component parts of nature and studied each in isolation, building the foundations of modern reductionism. Nature as a machine still suggested a Supreme Being with "Intelligent Design" until the theory of evolution challenged it.

Descartes attempted to understand the human soul within this mechanistic framework and this dualism persists today. That is, he reasoned on everything from first principles but as Malik says, "Few ideas have more shaped the modern imagination than his belief in the duality of body and soul." However, less reference is made to the many different concepts of self and our sense of 'me'. Our notions of the differences are very difficult to grasp until we accept that they are historically and culturally created.

Eric: Why then, is there no consensus when "all has been revealed"? Philosophers and social scientists, on the other hand, debate the nature of human subjectivity without considering its rootedness in biology. This has led to both sides failing to understand what makes us human. That is why I think that we need to return to a unity of approach with "joined-up" studies of history, politics, science and society. Do you agree?

Ray: We could argue about that but also about whether or not human history is progressive. In 1940 T.S. Elliot prophetically wrote, 'A good deal of our material progress is a progress for which succeeding generations may have to pay dearly.' Our personal progress and material advancement may be hiding the unpalatable fact that the planet will no longer be able to accommodate and adapt to the massive pressures on its ecosystem without dire consequences to its human population. If this is so, we may now be entering a new situation in which we should think in terms of 'One step forward, two steps back' and challenge the notion of inevitable progress. Following the period of the Enlightenment from the 18th century, the 19th saw rapid industrial and social changes to the accompaniment of a better future for all mankind. However, the horrors of the 20th century generated a general disillusionment about our global future.This is the theme running through my mind as I make these comments, but we should be optimistic in our ability, at least, to make this one step forward - to light a candle instead of cursing the darkness.

Eric: But don't we have experts and politicians capable of making the necessary decisions?

Ray: Maybe, but we also assumed that 'leaders', especially on the left, would know how to use their power wisely. Surely they would work in the interests of the vast majority and not only of themselves and an elite? Surely priority would be given to a more equitable distribution of vastly increased resources? Our aim then, as today, was to rectify the obscenity of widespread poverty and misery of a world in which twenty-six per cent of its population takes ninety-six per cent of its health resources and seventy four per cent of the world's population has to make do with only four per cent of health resources.

Eric: But every year brings an improvement.

Ray: Unfortunately the opposite is the case. Such glaring inequalities are increasing, and those in a position to redistribute wealth on a fairer basis, whether in government or on the boards of transnational corporations, seem to be intent on doing just the opposite despite the well-publicized largesse of Carnegie and others. They claim that only market forces can enable society to function and that people must be motivated by money and power. The role of interest groups, vested in perpetuating their power and privilege, was illustrated by the showing of an advert on one American TV station in 1996 by a conservation organisation. The advert was then refused by all the other stations because it showed a greedy, belching pig rising from a map of America - an image too near the truth for the business community to tolerate: 'Freedom' for the 'haves' to keep the 'have-nots' ignorant!

Eric: Perhaps we are what we are and nobody really understands what we are about! Human behaviour is what it is and we may as well live with it and get on with it.

Ray: That seems to me to be too fatalistic and I don't think that should be the case. Consider the comparative contributions of nature and nurture in determining what we are. First of all we are a product of our one hundred thousand genes unfolding a blueprint of every aspect of ourselves. Everybody can appreciate that my gender has been genetically determined. I am not bald because neither my father nor grandfather was bald. Not so obviously, I have certain mental and emotional traits which, on further examination, must have been inherited also. An even more interesting characteristic is my behaviour. As Helena Cronin has said, in *A Matter of Life and Death*: 'The clue to understanding our behaviour is to understand the rules of natural selection as laid down by our brains.' (See the appendix for a fuller discussion of the origins of our behaviour)

Eric: However, our personal identities, aspirations and achievements vitally depend on our experiences. No two people have the same set of experiences, so the possibility of cloning will produce 'look-alikes' with quite different characters, that is, they will be quite distinct and unique people.

Ray: I am not a Social Darwinist. There is no predestination but to what extent do we have free-will? The crucial issue, in my humble opinion, is that we are born 'unfinished' with a tremendous capacity to learn and a great potential to be proactive. Our genetic code gives us this potential to react in very complex ways to everything and everybody around us. From this, we construct our own particular identity out of the interaction of a multiplicity of factors; but how few people realise their full potential? How many go through life on 'automatic'? Another interesting point is that there is a mismatch between what our genes were designed to do in the days of palaeolithic man, and what our sophisticated social environment demands of us today, as we sit, imagine a hereafter, watch television and eat junk food instead of hunting, gathering and fighting for mere survival. In those days we had to be greedy to survive, whereas now it leads to the opposite.

TAPE THREE: THE PERSONAL IS POLITICAL

Eric: I was getting a bit tired of the monologue so I stopped the tape. Instead of coffee we had a dram of single malt. "Was it worth it?" I asked. Ray pondered. As he grew older he went in for more and more pondering. I asked, "You are getting away from the personal. What about yourself in all this?" "I guess so," he said in a low voice; not his usual assertiveness. "I may not have changed the course of events but I feel I was honest with myself." Ray would have chained himself to some railings for a cause even if he had to steal the railings. If Man is a political animal, Ray was the T-Rex of the ideological fauna. "So is the world now a better place? Was it worth it?" I repeated, following Paxman's technique. "Personally or politically?"

Ray: "I repeat again that the personal is political," Ray's sincerity saved him from pomposity. "Take the thirties for instance. I'm old enough to remember that the Great Depression was ending around 1936. It must have been true since the Government and the press said so! - yet my father was thrown out of work when the firm went bust."

Eric: Oh come on, Ray: There must have been plenty of jobs even if only due to rearmament. And what about new industries? Lots of folk were buying little cars, wireless sets, to say nothing of fridges, electric fires - I could go on with a whole list.

Ray: What good was that for men such as the miners or workers skilled in industries in decline! There was no other job and Dad became more depressed as the weeks and then the months went by. My father was seen on the Birkdale and Ainsdale golf courses as a caddie; some days lucky, some days not. Once, at the time of the Ryder Cup, I went with him to hand out leaflets from the club to the crowd of spectators. This was the only time I played truant and I felt guilty that my mother had to write an absence note that was a blatant lie.

Eric: "But who gave a toss. In fact, what made the news in those God-awful papers?" Ray gave a mirthless laugh. "Let me see," he said, "I remember helping Mum collect for 'Milk for Spain' when the Spanish Civil War was front-page news. But the real sensation was pictures of the Queen's new hat. Anyway let's finish this tape because I think we are at the point of being enlightened about my reflections on our early life." I pressed the button to finish the tape…

Eric: I'm obviously a product of the whole of my life history since conception and it is exceedingly difficult to tease out which characteristic is due solely to my genes and which to an environmental impact. We do not resemble cabbages growing up passively in a field. We are able to take initiatives and influence others as we are influenced by them, but don't many people leave it to 'them' to decide how the community is organised?

Ray: They may also see politicians as seeking power merely on their own behalf and being corrupted in the process. I viewed the world differently but I know that I abrogated my own responsibility in not seeking a career in politics. My first love was education, but I was not a mere 'voyeur' of the political scene. I was involved as a 'back-room boy' in the machines that people and their families take seriously from the local to the global. The grand project of socialism may have been put on the back burner or dropped altogether by most of its protagonists, but I am satisfied that, on balance, there was a constructive outcome to my deliberations - but that is a very subjective judgement.

Eric: What has been your political interest that has lasted the longest?

Ray: From the days of my active service in the Atlantic convoys during the war to my retiral as organiser of the Edinburgh Peace Festivals fifty years later, I was engaged in various peace movements and that is a cause of great satisfaction and humility - but not complacency. I believe that these concerted efforts by a great many people were instrumental in preventing an East-West conflict and made it difficult, for example, for the pro-nuclear lobby to sell the 'first-strike' policy. It should also stop the likes of Bush and Blair from again declaring war on the basis of a hidden agenda. Then I joined the Green Party and Democratic Left Scotland with many more issues.

Eric: So can we move on to your political life as you remember it?

Ray: I would like to record some thoughts and actions as an example of what very many of my generation experienced. That is why I think it is social history and not merely autobiographical. Hitherto, the personal and the political have rarely been brought together as two sides o coin. I have already mentioned that they are usually pigeonho separately. One has only to look at television programmes or books shelves of any library to see what I mean. The two topics are dealt w being mutually exclusive, and most people drift through life in a coc which is only motivated by their personal needs. It seems to me, howeve that we can only live a full life if we engage our personal demands within a social and political context. Indeed, I have found that life is much more interesting, understandable and satisfying if we know we belong to one another and act accordingly. This is not altruism. It is in our long-term enlightened self-interest.

Eric: What do you think is important for others to know about? Give me an idea how you tick because your conversations always seem to move away from the individual and particular and move directly to the political. Why?

Ray: Although my emotions and feelings have been deep and intense as an individual, invariably my thoughts have been social and my actions political. I have been concerned about the community of interest we have as human beings, in the family, as one of a crew or academic department, and through to the more obvious common concerns of organisations. I deemed the decision-making by these groups as political with a small 'p', not to be confused with 'party political' as the vehicle to obtain real power.

Eric: In this regard let us look at what you mean by security? This is a much used word by governments to defend unpopular decions.

Ray: It is felt very deeply by some and at the back of the mind by most, whether in the street, at home or in the workplace. People are made to think that it is only a personal problem as exemplified and reinforced by the ideology of pretending it to be a "slice of life" of the TV soap 'Coronation Street' which, in its many hundreds of episodes, has never referred to any social dimension, let alone collective action as in trades unions or political movements, even when there is an illegal sacking of workers or criminal activity. In contrast, security as a political issue is discussed by the authoritative voices of the well-kent faces, as the Scots would say of well-known people, of those in power and in the media, as though it were merely a party political football to be kicked around by 'those who understand such affairs'and a golden excuse to erode our human rights under an increasingly centralised and secretive system.

Eric: Sorry to interrupt but can we change the subject back to the individual?

Ray: Yes, sure. but it is novels that talk about particular individuals.

tors of the social and political scene are now current emphasis on individualism and market rs in society, have devalued the idea of John d' and enhanced Margaret Thatcher's famous ater, that 'There is no such thing as society'. elfish gene has, in my opinion, led to increased espect and trust in one's fellow human beings and, in agmentation of society, an increase in confrontation, divorce, , poverty and drugs; indeed, it had led to the alienation of the individual from a coherent view of a supportive system around him and to a big increase in the feeling of insecurity.

Eric: Are we, then, becoming a nation of ignorant slobs, victims of media and advertising hype, unwilling to serve anyone but ourselves?

Ray: Don't be so cynical! However, many young people boast that 'What matters in life is to look after number one', but even if it can be argued that most people avoid the responsibility of leadership, the social animal in man cannot be suppressed and will flourish in the right political environment. That, in a nutshell, is why I think that the personal is political but, of course, life is far more complicated than that. Our personal identity and self-worth are shaped by others. We are biologically autonomous but as social beings we need to co-operate within cohesive groups. If we cannot participate we cannot function properly and everybody suffers. It seems to me, therefore, that we operate within man-made, and not heaven-made, value systems and that our lifestyle depends on our place within these frames of reference just as our opinion of other road users depends on whether we are in the street as a pedestrian, a car driver, a cyclist or a bus passenger as mentioned above. We can change this role several times a day, and amusingly express different opinions, but we don't have much chance to change our social class, race, gender, religion, occupation or age!

Eric: These comments don't prove anything. They only serve to indicate that you habitually connect personal problems with the social and political. Most people don't, so what is it in your life that has determined this?

Ray: Not long ago I went to the consultant with a hernia and was told that it was not life-threatening so the waiting time was 18 months, but if I wanted to go private (that is, to pay for it), he could do it the following week.To me this is personal and at the same time a highly political problem namely the rights and wrongs of a two tier system of health depending on ability to pay. Of course, it would be less challenging to say how you would help someone on the NHS waiting list than to engage in a detailed discussion of Government policies and budgets.

Eric: So why don't our political representatives solve the problem?

Ray: For a politician, a sound bite and a slogan for the media seems to get the required reaction in their re-election.. Nowadays the main political parties use deep psychological studies of individuals in many small focus groups in which representative samples of the population are confronted with a variety of problems. Not merely what they say, but also their behaviour and body language are closely watched and analysed. Using this information, political parties then spend millions on the appropriate phrases and adverts to shape public opinion in order to achieve an elected dictatorship to further their interests.We then call this that much abused word "democracy". There is a case for a delegate type of "bottom up" democracy whereby M.Ps are elected by proportional representation, are mandated by local referenda or meetings to vote in a particular way in Parliament for members of the Cabinet who, in turn, elect the Prime Minister. What we have now is appointment by the Queen of the Prime Minister who then hires and fires his "yes men" to a Cabinet, and is not even anwerable to his party or nation and can decide what is debated in Parliament. That's an elected dictatorship, not a participatory democracy that we so urgently need.

Eric: You seem to be making generalisations again. Can I remind you that politics is the art of the possible in what some describe as a conservative, consumerist and pleasure-seeking Britain or, at least, the typical "Essex Man" or "Middle-Englander" that Blair was able to capture. Time has moved on, has it not?

Ray: Yes, they certainly have in the developed world. It is true that the left has been slow in realising the significance of these sociological changes. I agree that in the past we have given too much credence to abstract notions of what we would like human beings to be, rather than what they have become. This refers to the whole of the Labour Movement in Britain including the Trades Unions.

Eric: The history and problems of the CPGB before it dissolved itself are issues I'd like you to comment on from your own point of view. Perhaps we had better leave that for a later tape. In the meantime there is another aspect of the personal and the political. Can you, for instance, comment on the dilemmas you faced when you were politically active in opposing Government policies?

Ray: It is true that I have often walked the tightrope with an uneasy balance between the political and personal demands of the moment, but my convictions have led me to accept the dilemmas. My deep involvement may have been at the expense of my personal relationships and I can understand my family and friends subscribing to that. I tried to follow what I thought was for the greatest good, but you are at liberty to point out that the road to hell is paved with good intentions. So, some of us who have led such busy lives that we have not had 'time to stand and stare' now question everything. Until I was early retired these doubts were rhetorical, but then a number of influences coincided. I was approaching the end of my working life against a background of fast-moving global and national events. At the same time, I was able to pay more attention to more personal and leisure options that were opening up in front of me. At last I started to reflect on why I thought as I did that seemed at variance with others around me.

TAPE FOUR: BAGGAGE FROM THE PAST

Eric: For my sins I live alone but it has its compensations. I listen to Radio Three or one of my many CD's without being disturbed. I think. I reflect. I contemplate. It's my idea of heaven but Ray rang the bell. "So, can we hear Tape 4 about your memories as a child and your family background?" I said, in the hope that it might inform me of the origin of his politics. He put on the next tape himself, saying, "So you want me to write my autobiography." I didn't answer but just pointed to the recorder beside him.

Ray: As I have already said, I was named Ray Newton after I was born into a working-class part of Southport on February 21st, 1927. I feel as though I started life as only one of a family and not necessarily an important part - the typical middle child syndrome.From what I knew, I had only one living grandparent, my father's father, John Harry Newton, who lodged with the family. J.H. had been disinherited when his pub-owning father had left everything to his third wife, Charlotte, when he died in 1901. My parents met in Liverpool and lived in a flat there until 1924 when they moved to Southport. My father, Bob, left school at fourteen, unqualified to do anything and was eventually called up into the army towards the end of the First World War, then called the Great War, and served in the occupying force in Germany after it. He then picked up a job as office boy with a shipping company. My mother, Alice, didn't get on with her parents; she was five years older than her husband and had little schooling, mainly because she had been hospitalised with rheumatic fever for two years. However, she managed to leave home at fourteen by staying with her married sister and was found to be good at the jobs she undertook. Alice used to boast that by inventing her age she became an inspector of munitions during the war, but she was thrown out of work when 'the boys came home'. She was cut off by her parents in Darlington, having rejected their attempts to control every aspect of her life under the banner of Roman Catholicism and conservative values. Her two uncles had been killed in the war and she was told that it was God's will to defend king and country. There was unemployment, poverty and civil strife, especially in Liverpool, where even the police were on strike and the army had been drafted in. All this in a land she was told was 'fit for heroes to live in' yet, as a woman, she was not entitled to vote. That made her think! So the struggle to get a home together and the blatant injustices meted out to otherwise honest and hardworking individuals made it a political household, full of purposeful activity and conversation. There was, then, an exact date and place on my birth certificate, but no precise beginning to my function as a human being, no *tabula rasa*, no point zero, only a process of development interacting with other processes. The resulting form we call an individual, with an observable identity that we can describe but rarely understand. There are many times when we think we have cracked the nut only to discover a kernel which becomes more complicated as we try to peel off one layer after another until we realise it's a tear-jerking onion and we've bitten off more than we want to chew. Like all toddlers I must have interacted at every waking moment with everything and everybody around me. The very young human brain is one of great potential as it is only partially wired up, unlike the ready-made computers housed in lower life-forms. The millions of signals flowing into the sense receptors are filtered according to some internal value system. The resulting neural connections form patterns and structures possessed of meaning enabling me, for example, to develop a strategy of living. We now know that these early memories combine to produce a representational model of the world around us with which further inputs are compared and decisions made. That real world is the same for all, but the individual models of it are differentbecause our experiences of it are different, that is, we become selective. The wonder is, not that inconsistencies and confusions often occur, but that so much consensus is derived from apparent chaos.

Eric: This seems just the wisdom of the present. Who is a reliable witness to all this?

Ray: Yes, a good point; evidence is distorted by hindsight, partial knowledge and wishful thinking, as any judge will tell you. I am less than certain about my first recollections but I remember being told about the Italian invasion of Abyssinia, the Japanese in China and Hitler coming to power in 1933 when I was only six. Of course, it could well be that they were merely new names without significance but I certainly remember receiving a new penny coin with 1933 on it. There was also continual political comments made by my parents and I overheard the neighbours telling my mother that it was pretty useless talking to children about that sort of thing. These remarks stuck with me and I wanted to know more. Where was Germany? What did the Japanese look like? Were the Italians always cruel? I remember coming out of a shop in Chapel Street with my mother talking about the horrors of the 'Great War', as it was then called. Husbands of two of her sisters never came back. I imagined all sorts of scenarios and wondered about my own survival and whether we would be involved in yet another war.

Eric: Did you feel afraid and could it be that it was then embedded in your memory?

Ray: To a certain extent yes, but interestingly, these feelings were replaced in my teens by those of immortality - the norm for boys and young men who then engaged in dangerous activities as though death only happens to others. This is, of course, a sign of immaturity, but it is surprising that well-educated adults who know that man has invented gods and not the other way round, don't make a connection to a leaf rotting underneath a tree, and then conclude that we shall also disappear in the recycling process, together with our minds and souls. We always seem desperately keen to delude ourselves. Of course, the tragedy of human existence is that we know of our own demise and we don't like it. No doubt wishful thinking about immortality is a necessary prop for some people, but it doesn't make it true.

Eric: Let's go back to the way your interest in politics was influenced as a child.

Ray: It was my parents, especially my mother, who were the key influences, directing my attention to what was happening in the rest of the world. Never a day passed without their comments on global and national affairs, and this seemed to be at variance with what was happening in other families. Therefore, we seemed to be swimming against the tide of conventional wisdom, and to that extent life was difficult. Unlike the other people in the street my parents went to political meetings and visitors to the house talked about the headline news and what was happening to the unemployed. I remember the 1935 general election and a candidate called Carrington. The kids at school had screwed up rolls of newspaper on long pieces of string which they swung round over their heads and into the faces of anybody who was going to vote Labour, so I kept my trap shut. These were working-class children, but they lived in an area devoid of working-class solidarity, unlike the mining and industrial communities. Southport was a seaside resort with seasonal labour, mainly servicing, and was a safe Tory seat. The executives commuting to Liverpool and Manchester were looked on as their betters - a different class of people.

Being Protestant and royalist seemed to be the natural order of things and the children were happy if they were given bread and taken to circuses. I was very conscious that my parents were trying to change things and that evil triumphs if good people do nothing, so I grew up with a sense of purpose in a challenging atmosphere that the future was all to play for on the basis of making two steps forward for every one we were pushed back. It was 1936 and the Great Depression was ending. At least that was what the Government and the press were saying at the time, but my father was thrown out of work when the firm went into liquidation. At first, talk in the family was about alternative employment, even drawing us all into the conversation to provide a melting-pot of suggestions. No doubt this was a ploy to shield us from the truth. There was no other job and Dad became more depressed as the weeks and then the months went by. My father was then seen on the Birkdale and Ainsdale golf courses as a caddie; some days lucky, some days not.

Eric: But what do you remember specifically before the war. After all you were only in Primary school and not a student of world affairs?

Ray: 1936 and subsequent years remain vivid in my memory; helping Mum collect for 'Milk for Spain' when the Spanish Civil War was front-page news, together with pictures of the Queen's new hat. We also went to the Co-op field days where there were bags of buns, three-legged races and bands playing. At one in particular mother spoke through the public address system and showed me a different side to her character, a confident and persuasive speaker. Up till then there were separate men's and women's guilds. My parents founded the Mixed Guild, mother as president and father as secretary, and this was the reason that a typewriter and a table of correspondence permanently occupied a corner of the sitting-room. In the summer of 1937 mother went to the Soviet Union as the Lancashire representative of the Co-op guilds, and was then invited to speak all over the county to talk about it. I was secretly proud of her new-found importance, but I was reticent in my own comments to friends as it was not the received wisdom of the moment and I was caught between being thought of as 'odd' and my desire to be identified as typical of my peer group. However, it did establish in my mind that my parents' contribution to the work of organisations added value to their worth and it never occurred to me that it also meant less time devoted to us children. Doing our own thing was the norm.

Eric: Now that I've understood more of your background, let us get to your political side. Did you consciously think of the politics of the time or were they just comments and memories as a series of pictures of family life?

Ray: In general both. I found it easier to be conventional in some things in order to admit that I was a labour supporter. My parents were actually in the Left Book Club and members of the Communist Party of Great Britain (CPGB). Because Dad was out of work he used to collect copies of the *Daily Worker* from Chapel Street Station each morning to deliver to about 20 houses. The wholesalers wouldn't handle them and occasionally the bundle was found on the railway lines, thrown there by the very workers they were trying to help. Accompanying my dad probably gave me more political education than any number of lectures. I also read the leaflets that Dad gave me to distribute round the houses nearby so I became well versed in campaigning in the 'struggle for socialism'. At that time priority was given in the movement to the threat from the rise of Fascism in Europe and the 'neutral' policy of the British Government allowing Franco, Hitler and Mussolini to expand their territory and power. The policy of 'non-intervention' in Spain was, in fact, tacit support for Franco. There was more overt support for Hitler and Mussolini to ban trades unions and arrest the communists, at least by the *Daily Mail*, which seemed at the time to have been given an undeserved status like *The Times*.

Eric: What are the key issues you remember of the wartime years?

Ray: I was only twelve when the war broke out, yet I remember the political contexts and events, as described and explained by my mother on an almost daily basis. With hindsight, the analyses were remarkably accurate and poignant, and are etched permanently on my memory. For example, when Chamberlain came back from a meeting with Hitler in Munich, waving a piece of paper and declaring 'Peace in our time' the press and radio hailed it as a victory for the government. The newsreels on the cinema screens showed the grateful and cheering population, but my mother explained that this was all wrong. It was an attempt, she said, to encourage Hitler to expand eastwards without interference from the west but there was a difference of emphasis. Some like Churchill and Boothroyd saw that Hitler's ambitions were boundless and would affect the interests of Britain and the Empire. Others wanted to be friendly and accommodating to Hitler hoping that would keep us out of the war and therefore dismissed proposals for an alliance of countries bordering Germany to stop any further expansion. Britain specifically refused to sign a mutual defence pact with France and the Soviet Union that would have attempted to contain Hitler. So the Soviet Union made a non-aggression pact with Germany, not, as is sometimes portrayed, a mutual defence pact, but in order to gain time before the inevitable onslaught. Later, when Hess, Hitler's deputy, parachuted on to Lord Hamilton's estate in Scotland, my mother immediately explained that his mission was to sue for non-intervention by the British as the Germans prepared to attack Russia.

Eric: Are you sure you remember all this? As they say - hindsight can be a wonderful thing but is retropective from the information you have acquired since.

Ray: I remember this clearly, as I thought at the time it was rather odd for my mother to have such detailed information that wasn't currently expressed in the news. I wondered why none of my classmates were privileged enough to have had that analysis, though it is now generally accepted and perhaps enhanced rather than weakened by the Government's decision to keep the list of Hess's contacts top secret, 'in the national interest', beyond the normal fifty-year rule. Historians now concur with my mother's explanation!

Eric: You can imagine that my Jewish family had realised that very difficult times lay ahead. Times must have been hard on your family but for different reasons.

Ray: To all those who suffered indescribable misery during the war it may seem incongruous that my family, like many others, suddenly enjoyed a rise in their standard of living and even their quality of life. My father got a job. Money came into the house. Rationing meant not so much a restriction as an invitation to buy a whole range of food and goods that we weren't able to afford before the war. The full rations were bought and Dad sold the bacon to Mr Ball the insurance man who called every Saturday morning. Like many other working-class people my parents only insured for funerals lest the ignominy of a pauper's grave awaited them. For the first time there was a radio in the house - a cheap brown Bakelite one tuned in for most of the time to the Home Service of the BBC, but sometimes to the Light Programme with Tommy Handley's ITMA, *Workers' Playtime*, *Happidrome* or *Music Hall.* Such programmes certainly brought laughter into the house and there was an added quality of listening together. With a bit of knob twiddling it was possible to hear Lord Haw-Haw's 'Germany calling, Germany calling'. This English traitor gave details of events not broadcast by the BBC, but with plausible comments to establish his credibility, such as details of bombing raids. This would be followed by some opinions of his own with an easy conversational manner and then stone-biting criticism of Britain's war effort which would be a topic of discussion in the playground the following morning. Life for me was actually very enjoyable.

Eric: Today we are saturated with media coverage of one sort or another. What was the main source of news and comment, daily papers or the radio?

Ray: Definitely the radio, with two channels, both BBC. You must remember that the BBC was very much an arm of the Government of the day and only the plummy accents of the public school came over the air in the serious programmes and news items. Regional accents were reserved for comedy, but there was a near revolution of the middle classes when the Yorkshireman Wilfred Pickles was brought in to read the news and gave the press a lot to comment on. The *Daily Worker* was banned and other newspapers were censored. *Movietone News* in the cinema was meant to raise morale with a lot of pseudo-patriotic charm. Labour had joined a National Government, but it was Churchill and Boothby who led the debate against Chamberlain's war policies which in turn led to his fall from grace. Churchill's eloquence over the radio was important in the new prosecution of the war with his promise of 'blood, toil, tears and sweat' and, as a result, the population was given a clearer sense of purpose and direction.

Eric: I'm trying to understand how you were thinking as a child. Let's get personal again with what you recall from those days as a junior school pupil.

Ray: Everybody had been provided with a gas mask in a cardboard box. Most people made a better carrying case and shoulder strap and it was carried night and day wherever we went. I volunteered to take a weekend course and was told how to paste strips of paper on the window to counteract the effects of flying glass. I had already read about such measures in the leaflets that could be picked up in the libraries and the newly formed community centres, but the practical side was completely new and I got a great deal of satisfaction tackling the burning magnesium of an incendiary device with a long-handled rake and pan. Another exercise was the use of sand and stirrup pumps against fires and finally, with my rubber-faced gas mask with its carbon-filled canister, walking through an air-locked passage of tear gas. Those who hadn't got their gas masks on snug around their face soon knew about it, including big, tough men exiting with their eyes streaming! This was amusing but in a real situation it could have been mustard gas and quite a different story.

Eric: Keep to the personal and give me a picture of the day to day scene?

Ray: The blackout was rigorously enforced by the wardens knocking on the door if there was even the smallest chink of light. At home in Bedford Road only the living-room was regularly used and blacked out. There was usually a coal fire and the back boiler heated the hot water. As this was the only warm room the whole family congregated there. In winter the bedrooms were cold, but a hot plate from the oven was put into the bed for about ten minutes before getting into it. Adding your vest and socks to your pyjamas also helped. This happened to be useful when a landmine dropped nearby, blew in the front windows and we were taken downstairs for the night, wrapped in coats and spare blankets. Cheap translucent glass replaced the broken panes, but this was the least of the family worries and did not warrant even a discussion the following morning. Of continuing concern was the political situation, but, like most children entering their teens, money was needed for the increasing demand for clothing and leisure, so I found a Saturday job as an errand boy at Hoyles the grocer's. During the Liverpool blitz the van driver who delivered the bread from the central bakery told of the previous night's bombing, and how he had spent the night dragging out casualties and fighting the fires as an auxiliary. At this time civilians and merchant seamen were suffering more than those in the forces as the land war was at a standstill as Hitler was building up to attack Russia.

Eric: Were you personally in any danger?

Ray: None of my family was directly affected but amongst my abiding memories are the ack-ack guns firing and shells exploding in mid-air, the tell-tale 'wow-wow' droning of the German bombers, the searchlights criss-crossing the night sky, the orange glow in the direction of Liverpool and then the ghostly silence after the all-clear had been sounded, followed by an uneasy sleep. Knowledge of bombed sites and wrecked planes were shared between pupils the next day, and some brought souvenirs to prove the point. My father took his turn at fire-watching in Liverpool and also did a spell assisting the anti-aircraft crews as a member of the Home Guard. One night he had a meeting so he swapped with a colleague. Returning from work the next day he described how a bomb had gone down the lift shaft of the building he was scheduled to fire-watch, demolishing the entire building, so he spent the day helping to set up a temporary office elsewhere.

Eric: People must have been anxiousy and grumbling about the difficulties.

Ray: Not really. Everybody accepted the difficulties but, of course, there was a common goal and a sense of purpose pervading everyday life. The superficial was differentiated from the meaningful. The popular view of political events closely followed that of the press and the radio, but my mother frequently gave a different interpretation. She called it a 'class analysis' because of the clash of interest between those who worked by hand and brain for a wage and those who owned the wealth and were able then to dictate economic policy. The establishment used the media and the state machine to perpetuate their privileged position. Therefore, according to my mother, the working class had got to be organised to defend themselves or they would just be kept down; by the same measure the poor would get poorer and the rich would get richer. Politics was not, therefore, just a matter of personality clashes, a view beloved by journalists and historians, but of individuals attempting to survive and throwing up social movements in the process.This made sense to me, even though jargon, sectarianism and dogmatism crept into the arguments, so I joined the Young Communist League which met every Monday evening in the town centre. Sometimes there was a good speaker and a knowledgeable chairperson, but this was not often, and the discussion centred on the most assertive characters there, which kept me quiet.

Eric: The Soviet-German pact of non-tervention gave Hitler a breathing space. As a communist family you must have particular memories of Russia joining the War.

Ray: Unfortunately Stalin thought it would give him a chance to rearm. However, on the morning of June 21st, 1941 the radio announced that Germany had attacked the Soviet Union without warning or declaring war, and along the whole two thousand mile front. My parents went immediately to the local branch secretary of the Communist Party, as they felt that there was a real possibility of Britain standing aside to let them fight it out which is what Lord Vansittart had advised the government after Hess's flight to Lord Hamilton 's estate. To Churchill's great credit he declared that fascism was the main enemy and therefore Russia would be an ally in that fight. The phoney war had ended. Everyone was galvanised into action by a united labour and trades union movement. Britain was no longer alone and it became possible to imagine the defeat of fascism.

Eric: Did your friends talk about the War?

Ray: At school, the talk was of the length of time it would take for Russia to surrender. There were various estimates from a few weeks to a few months depending on which commentator or journalist you listened to. A teacher, Mr Williams, opened a discussion on the topic. Some of the pupils said a fortnight, reflecting on the blitzkriegs across the countries of Europe. Others thought it might take up to three months as the distances involved were greater. As I was shaking my head at all these suggestions 'Taffy' asked me to come to the front and give my opinion. I explained why the war game had now changed and that Russia would never surrender. Mr Williams tried to quell the loud guffaws of disbelief at Nutcase Newton voicing such idiocies. Time went by, six months, then a year. Then the Germans were being pushed back and I gave a wry smile as Mr Williams reminded the class of what was said at the discussion at the end of the summer term in 1941. There was a campaign for the West to open a second front and both Stalin and Roosevelt talked about the need for this. Churchill, however, procrastinated and went for the so-called 'Soft under-belly of the Axis' in the Mediterranean, with long supply lines and difficult terrain, especially in Italy where my schoolboy friend Ralph

Keeley's two brothers, Jim and Jack, were killed. At the time, the news of someone being killed in action was quickly put out of one's mind. It was only much later that it struck me that I was enjoying an interesting life and that these poor suckers had none of it. In the conference season of 1943 I joined a demonstration for the second front when the news came through of the 'invasion' of Dieppe, but elation soon turned to sadness as it transpired that it had been merely an exploratory landing and that many Canadians had been killed for apparently very little reward.

Eric: How did the war progress in terms of victories and defeats in battle?

Ray: This is not a history of the war. Its annals have been well documented elsewhere. Like everyone else I had my own experiences and attitudes and was well aware that an optimistic gloss was being put on all news items for public consumption - and why not? A government must generate support and unify the nation in its common task of defeating fascism. There was also a simple logic that there must be a silver lining to every cloud and a sunny spell after every thunderstorm, so people had a right to expect happier times to come. On the other hand, if this kind of propaganda is overplayed, it can be counterproductive and cynicism develops, destroying people's moral fibre.

Eric: You must have witnessed a lot of depressed people around you at the time.

Ray: It may come as a surprise to you that I didn't. Compared to pre-war, there was an increasing sense of community and friendship, of mutual help and sharing. There must have been crime but it was not much in evidence and I cannot remember any vandalism. Neither do I remember the back door of the house being locked, but some people had padlocks on their bikes and removed the lamp when leaving it.Thus, the norms of human behaviour were established in my mind during my schooldays but in a wartime situation there is another ingredient. The resilience of the population is enormously helped by an external value system that goes beyond the welfare of the individual. Community values are enriched and the mental health and the quality of life of all are enhanced. I naively thought that these social attitudes would develop further into a socialist framework of society in the whole of Europe - 'from each according to his work; to each according to his need'. What went wrong?

Eric: That's not for me to answer. What I'd like to know is how much choice did young people have at that time especially in deciding their futer careers?

Ray: For most people it was a matter of survival and life had taught them to take opportunities where they existed. Take one day at a time and wait to be called up to join the armed forces. Yet there was a common aspiration and a common good which also entered into the equation. People were generally responsive to appeals to their better nature. For some it may have been lip-service, telling their friends in the pub of their good intentions and only a cynic would have bragged about the uselessness of doing anything for anybody. In other words, there was a common assumption that 'I am my brother's keeper' - or perhaps it was just a tradition of working-class solidarity to counter the ongoing insecurity.

Eric: But you left school at 16, applied to join the Merchant Navy, worked on a farm then on a building site. You then were asked to go on an Outward Bound course and was taken by Elder Dempster Lines as an apprentice or cadet for deck officer. Tell me about it. Was it as straightforward as I imagine anyone starting their working lives?

Ray: Well, yes it was and I was excited and looking forward as you can guess. I signed my indentures as an apprentice deck officer, or midshipman as it was formerly known, on my seventeenth birthday, 21st February 1944 and joined my first ship, the *SS Calumet* in Hull. It was a typical cargo ship of the time, eight thousand tons gross, built at John Brown's on the Clyde in 1927, the year that I was born. Unlike the majority of ships it was steam-turbined with firemen and stewards from West Africa. Altogether there were fifty-six crew, but eight of these were naval gunners for the twin marlin machine guns, the Oerliken anti-aircraft and the four-inch howitzer on the stern. There were no guns on the foredeck as that would have classified the ship as offensive instead of defensive and different rules of engagement would have applied.

Eric: What do you remember of those first weeks at sea?

The first experience of anything is etched permanently in the memory and then acts as a frame of reference which subsequent images amplify or modify. After a long trail out into the mid-Atlantic in convoy, going at the speed of the slowest, which was usually six knots, the *Calumet* arrived at Freetown in Sierra Leone, anchoring about a mile offshore. The panoramic view was straight out of the geography textbook, but ten times more detailed. What no photograph, film or description can convey are the smells, noise and general ambience of the scene. The air was humid and hot with sweat soaking and rotting each shirt on my back. A thought came to my teased mind. The olfactory nerve endings must be well-connected to the long-term memory areas of the brain, because the same smell or mixture of smells evokes the same visual scene and, by association, creates nostalgia.The next five trips were on the *David Livingstone*, a smaller diesel-engined cargo ship capable of carrying twelve passengers plus a doctor. On one occasion we left the convoy as it passed the latitude of the Canary Islands during the night and went into Tenerife at the port of Santa Cruz with a cargo of seed potatoes.

The people looked desperately poor, many of them barefoot and in rags. I got talking to an English-speaking tally clerk who told me that two German U-boats had left the night before. Spain was supposed to be neutral but was an ally of the Nazis, and the Canaries were isolated and its people starving.

Eric: Tell me what was happening on the home front in the war.

Ray: At home, there was a general acceptance of shortages, but I didn't see any real deprivation. It was now obvious that the allies were winning the war and morale was high with talk focused on 'after the duration'. There were Ministry of Information films and pamphlets, press features and talks on the radio about reconstruction. The Beveridge Report built up people's hopes and expectations of the prospect of a welfare state from the cradle to the grave, of new housing in neighbourhood units with libraries, nursery schools and community centres with youth clubs. There was going to be such a lot of work to be done that unemployment would be a thing of the past. Like millions of others, I contrasted this picture of the future with that of the poverty, unemployment and hopelessness of pre-war times. Thus there was a feeling of optimism in adversity, a sense of purpose in society at large, a feeling that people would matter, have an equal opportunity and that the struggles would be worthwhile. I remember reflecting, 'Does man have to have an enemy to get the best as well as the worst out of him?' In contrast to the end of the First World War there was no mood at all for monuments, only reconstruction of both buildings and people's lives. The Russians had conquered Berlin with terrible loss of life on both sides. The Americans met them as they advanced across the Rhine. The concentration camps were filmed and shown to cinema audiences, with names like Belsen and Auschwitz and a dozen others becoming symbols of man's inhumanity to man. Victory in Europe Day, VE day was declared on May 8th, 1945; the *David Livingstone* was anchored off the village of Abonema in the Niger Delta, loading mahogany logs.

Eric: So, peace at last! How did your daily routine change after the fighting stopped?

The war in the Pacific would continue for another three months, but everyone knew it was drawing to a close. One morning at breakfast in the saloon the message came through that an atomic bomb had been dropped on Hiroshima and had wiped it out. Initially there were cheers, but the conversation got round to the doubts about rivalries after the war. Japan was already suing for peace. Did this end the war in the Pacific or was it the opening shot of a third round of hostilities and showing the world which country was boss. I thought that the older men in the discussion were too cynical. We shall have a new international organisation, the United Nations, I said rather unconvincingly to those who remembered the old League of Nations. The next nuclear bomb on Nagasaki seemed to make even less sense as Japan was already suing for peace as the American battleships pounded the coast and Tokyo lay in ruins from massive bombing raids. Perhaps the new US President, Harry Truman, wanted to make sure the world knew his power, having half the world's resources and industrial production within his grasp.

Eric: As a matter of interest what was the method of payment at sea?

Ray: Sailors get paid off at the end of the voyage minus any regular payments sent to the family and bar bills spent at sea. At Liverpool the news came through that the 'danger money' would no longer be paid. This had been increased during the war instead of the basic so that take-home pay would plummet unless consolidated together. Now my remuneration, according to my indentures was nine pounds for the whole of the first year, twelve pounds for the second, fifteen pounds for the third and twenty-four pounds for the fourth, but the 'danger money' was one hundred and twenty pounds per year.There was a spontaneous outcry when the 'danger money' was stopped, and I was slightly bemused when even the most conservative cadets declared they wouldn't go to sea until the marine officers' union got 'their money back'! How the shipowners thought they could get away with it boggles the imagination. It was a complete throwback to their pre-war attitudes and practices. Needless to say the 'danger money' was then incorporated into the basic wage and the ships sailed again. They had to. The cargoes had to be shifted.

Eric: Can you recall more of the immediate post-war years - but wait a moment and I'll go and make another pot of tea!

Ray: I collected my three war medals and they were not to see the light of day until forty years later at a demo of ex-services CND. My next trip was a short one across to Antwerp when the battleship *Missouri* carried Truman on his way to the Potsdam Conference. The two cadets were invited to go on a day trip to Brussels by an assistant in the British consulate. We dined in the Officers' Club at the tables occupied only a few months earlier by SS officers and were served by the same waiters, together with the same orchestra. I had never witnessed such a lifestyle. In contrast, the dockers were given huge spam sandwiches to maintain their energy to unload the ships. Seeing big American cars and luxury goods going into the warehouses I inquired about the destinations. The tally clerks recognised the consignees as Belgians who had made a lot of money in the Belgian Congo but had it frozen 'for the duration'. The products? Copper and Uranium, of course! The assistant consul was becoming very friendly and spoke of the mega-rich having kept their heads down or having even collaborated, but that now they were re-establishing themselves in the hierarchy of pre-war connections to continue exactly where they left off. On the way back to London the sea was calm with a beautiful mackerel sky. The general election results were coming over the radio: a landslide victory for Labour. There was elation all around. I was even surprised by the skipper's reaction. There was no doubt about Churchill's popularity as a war leader, but he had been the only card that the Conservative Party had been playing, whereas the issues had been jobs, education, the health service and above all, housing, and Labour had concentrated on a discussion of these. The electorate may have been apprehensive about the underlying difficulties and possible solutions, but they were ready to face the hard task of reconstruction. Most elections are lost rather than won; that is, the incumbent government has failed to deliver and votes are cast against it rather than for an alternative. I believe that the 1945 election was different inasmuch as there was an all-pervading moral and cultural change demanding positive action. There was a flood of progressive ideas that would relegate conservatism to the dustbin of history, to be replaced by socialist policies.

Eric: But your parents were in the Communist Party, not the Labour Party. Wasn't the Communist Party irrelevant to the struggle for socialism in Britain?

Ray: No! The Communist Party proclaimed that the Labour Party had no overall strategy and principle although it was founded by the trade union movement and therefore gained the workers vote. It became a vehicle of achieving power for career politicians that meant it would give way under the pressures mounted by the defenders of the financial and industrial establishment. This was soon shown to be the case and even the newly nationalised industries of coal, gas, steel and the railways had boards appointed that saw their function to be that of underpinning and enriching the private sector. Foreign policy, especially under Bevin, became one of complete subservience to the United States. Willie Thomson, the Glasgow historian and writer friend, has a similar view of those post-war years: "Wealth distribution remained unaltered, but more importantly tied the country to the US Military chariot, and the British economy to the consequences of these choices set the agenda for the next fifty years, profoundly infected the cultural climate and ensured that the economic and political crisis of the Seventies was resolved in favour of the right and not the left. Labour, when it had been in office since 1945, had, no doubt, tried its best to govern in the interests of the country at large. It had been forced into crises on each occasion and ultimately out of office because the City had been unwilling to tolerate even the mild degree of intervention that these administrations tried to sustain. The Labour governments were left beleaguered and vulnerable to the electoral bloc which could be mobilised against them. *"New Times"*, 1996.

Eric: But that was a long time ago and this is only one man's opinion of a few facts.

Ray: I quote this because it succinctly echoes my view and also indicates how little has changed with the advent of New Labour. After the war the economic situation got worse rather than better. British assets had been sold to the United States in exchange for Marshall and the Empire's coffers were empty. The suppliers wanted hard currency and that meant dollars. Labour ministers then went cap in hand to the financiers who imposed conditions that made them subservient to their demands for belts to be tightened and social reform to be halted. Rationing was more widely applied. The mines and railways had deteriorated through lack of investment before the war and overuse during it. Industry continued with the same tooling and concentrated on the short-term promotion of exports, with only limited utility furniture and clothes available for the home market.

Eric: Surely there was a lot of progress. They founded the NHS and the welfare state.

Ray: Yes, the NHS was born and there was a lot of idealism in the air, but the wartime alliance of the USSR and ourselves was broken up, culminating in Churchill's Fulton speech. The cold war started, defence expenditure soared and not even the House of Commons was informed of the plans to build nuclear weapons. The hot war of British intervention in Greece, Malaya and India continued and Britain reverted to its role as an imperialist nation with a large contingent of forces in the five continents. It may have been a fiction during the war, but those who had wealth didn't seem to flaunt it. Now they did, but said they had no incentive to invest in British industry, so the Labour Government felt that they were in a catch-22 situation. Whose interest were they going to serve? Incentives had to be given to the financiers, but not to the working population, and strikes resulted.

Eric: What do you remember of what the Communist Party was doing?

Ray: During the war the Communist Party, of which my parents were members, gave priority to the strengthening of the trades unions and this paid dividends to working people after the war and many historians like Nina Fishman, now recognise this. We heard over the radio about the dockers and how they were holding the country to ransom, but nothing about the 'strike' of capital in failing to invest in socially desirable projects at home but instead invested abroad, so some (the rich) were given carrots and others (wage-earners) were given the stick. The electorate were becoming increasingly disillusioned and the Tory Housewives League went on the offensive with full press support, yet the Labour Party couldn't even produce a daily paper to present their interpretation of events and so backtracked on their promises.

Eric: But let's get back to your young life. How long did you stay in the merchant navy?

Ray: I had to stay 'on active service' until my "demob" number came up like everyone else on war service. My next ship was the *SS Cochrane*, the sister ship to my first, the *Calumet*, and sailed for a whole year between West Africa and the United States. The shops in Manhattan were full of consumer goods of all kinds, having been produced continuously throughout the war. When questioned, some Americans complained that they had to wait for their orders for a new car to come through, as though it were a terrible hardship. It is true that in the American press at the time there were reports of young couples having to sleep in their cars because they couldn't get a house, which rather amused me, knowing that all car production had stopped in Britain and that the pre-war tooling had then been brought out of storage to produce cars after the war like the old Ford Anglia and Prefect. To prevent profiteering the American Administration had controlled prices, but when I handed over the exact money for a bar of chocolate I was told to hand over another dime with the comment, 'If you don't want it you needn't have it', so it boiled down to market forces - if you had the money you could get anything! That is the way I was thinking at the time.

TAPE FIVE: THE HISTORICAL IS POLITICAL

Eric: I think your earlier life had a great influence on your subsequent political life so could you continue with your autobiographical approach. I understand that you applied for a course at a teaching college under the emrgency training scheme but when exactly was that?

Ray: O.K. In September 1949 I ended my sea service and entered the London Garnett College. .A fellow student, Ruth Massie, invited me to a meeting of the Hampstead branch of the Communist Party at which her father, Professor Hyman Levy, was speaking, and after reading one of his books I joined the party, but took no active role then as I was concentrating on my studies and preparation for teaching practice. The Korean War started in 1950 and the immediate effect at home was to send prices up. I bought some blankets as soon as I saw that the price of wool had shot up and it wasn't long before this was reflected in the shops. Seeing these blankets on our bed for the next twenty years never failed to remind me of the savings I had made. Of course, the Korean War was much more serious than that. Two million lives were lost and many more millions wrecked. The whole weight of the United States was now engaged in a 'hot war'. Stalin kept out of it as the USSR was still exhausted by the war. There was also increasing concern about the threats that were being made by the U.S. to drop nuclear weapons on the Chinese when they intervened and pushed the Americans back. What interested me at the time, and which has subsequently been vindicated as fact, is that Atlee, yearning for the alliance, made a dash across the Atlantic for an emergency meeting with the US President, to plead restraint on General MacArthur, who intended to drop nuclear weapons in order to defeat the Chinese. Later I was to hear Professor Ritchie-Calder give a 'blow-by-blow' account of the anguished Cabinet decision in the face of growing public concern especially within the ranks of the Labour Party, although at the time suggestions to this effect were being denied.

Eric: I seem to remember that but what was the role of the Soviet Union then?

Ray: Now that the archives of the Soviet Union have been opened up and are being studied, a fresh light is being shed on their handling of international affairs, and Paul Lashmar, a BBC producer, has reported that Stalin told Kim Il Sung that it was 'not advisable for North Korea to engage in offensive action against South Korea', despite the activities of the American-installed and 'aggressive nationalist leader, Sygman Rhee'. It is true that at the time, those of us on the left supported the Russian stance and opposed the American one on principle. Of course, the issues were not so black and white, but America had over one hundred and fifty bases encircling the Soviet Union and acted as the world's policeman. It was therefore important to defend the Soviet position when the whole of the establishment and the media were engaged in an hysterical campaign against it. *Realpolitik* is not an easy concept to handle, especially if we are not made aware that there is another side to the proganda coin.

Eric: But wasn't the United States were merely defending its national interest?

Ray: The archives of the United States are now being made available through their 'Freedom of Information Act', and a documentary on BBC2 in 1996, *Baiting the Bear*, told the story of General Curtis Le May's 'Project Control'. He was the Commander in charge of America's Strategic Air Command of nuclear bombers. Unknown to President Eisenhower, he had his finger on the nuclear button without the need for presidential clearance, and went ahead with overflying the Soviet Union, deliberately seeking a pretext for a nuclear attack. President Kennedy was horrified, but was told by Le May's deputy that he'd regard it as a victory if only one Russian and two Americans survived. Today we seem even luckier to be alive than we thought yesterday!

Eric: But Russia was also defending what it saw as its national interest.

Ray: It may be true that many of us were naive about 'Russian National Interests' but my opinion of those times does not differ much from the views I held then because the Cold War was in full swing. The free-for-all in the global market place was dominated by the United States, but the Soviet bloc was closed to it. The drive for maximum profits was also limited by socialist ideology and action in Europe, and John Foster Dulles proclaimed that the role of the West was to 'roll back Communism' and defeat the advance of socialism, especially in Italy, France and Britain. The Labour

Government had already declared its unquestioning loyalty to the White House, mainly for economic reasons, and had 'proved' itself with military action around the globe, as in Malaya, Greece, India, Kenya, Aden and other places 'in the national interest', a catch-all phrase when there's a hidden agenda in the interests of the wealthy few.At that time the United States announced a huge increase in 'defence' expenditure. It initiated the founding of NATO, insisting that it would always be headed by an American general 'to protect our national interests', as Congress put it. The Soviet Union responded likewise and the Warsaw Pact was formed. The arms race had begun which was eventually to bankrupt the Soviet Union. Those who had struggled against poverty and unemployment in the Thirties, had seen active service during the war and had suffered the privations after it, were now becoming disillusioned with the Government in which they had put their faith. I could see the dilemma of members of the Labour Party who wanted social progress but had to support a Labour Government which was increasing taxes to pay for rearmament, going back on its promises that then led to its defeat at the polls.

Eric: We hear very little of Britain in the Fifties. We seemed to recovering very slowly from the war. What was the general mood at the time? Had we, in fact recovered from the war? What do you remember of what you deem to be politically significant?

Ray: 1951 was the year of the great Festival of Britain, one hundred years after the Great Exhibition of 1851 which had heralded Britain's overwhelming dominance of world industrial production and trade. I went to see it while in London as there was already some controversy about it. It was supposed to mark the end of post-war gloom and the press hyped it up as the greatest ever. Yes, it was worth seeing, especially the displays of science and technology. However, I was disappointed in the cultural and political aspects with the kaleidoscope of oddments - our royal heritage to national orchestras, bagpipes and cricket. There was no social history nor vision of the future for the British people. There was a complete exclusion of the labour and trades union movement, yet it was a Labour Government that had commissioned and paid for it. It was just as if it had been put into the hands of Conservative Central Office to organise, with their nostalgia of the Empire and England's 'green and pleasant land', with a lot of stale ideas thrown in about the future of consumer growth as though that was the aim in life.

Eric: During the war the communist parties grew quite substantially to be quite influential. What happened after Truman and Churchill said in 1947 that our main enemy was the Soviet Union and the spread of communism but that was interpreted by different communist parties.

Ray: I remember well that 1951 was also the year of the publication of the Communist Party's *British Road to Socialism.* It marked a departure from the 'Comintern' days in that it described an independent and parliamentary way for Britain, whether or not this was appropriate for other countries. The Soviet Union was recognised as the 'leading force' because its collapse would inevitably be a defeat for all, so that no dirty washing was washed in public and international solidarity was regarded as the key to any progress anywhere. However, it was not so much the global as the local that energised the political campaigns, but by this time I was fully engaged in the building of my own future. Mary and I were married in August 1951 in Leeds and honeymooned near Grantham. This was one month after my brother, John, had graduated as a doctor, and had emigrated to the States as an intern at a hospital in Trenton, New Jersey. On a more important aspect, before the war only four per cent of the population owned a car. In 1950 there were three million on the road. By 1980 this had risen to twenty million, and we are now locked into a car culture that is a threat instead of an asset. What do I remember of 1956? An increasing number of cars were being produced in Britain and imported cars were a novelty and expensive. There was a waiting list which varied according to the model; about eight months for a Morris Minor, my first choice, and five months for an Austin A30. There were models like the Ford Prefect, in which the driving school had taught me to pass the test, and there were pre-war designs when the machine tools were put to one side and resurrected afterwards.There was suddenly a new interest in higher education by the Establishment after years of resistance to any form of expansion. The space firsts by the Soviet Union had sent shock waves around the educational and political institutions of the West. The question was asked in the media and elsewhere - how could a nation, not long after it had been devastated by war and then isolated in peace, catch up, let alone overtake the USA which had, in contrast, come out of the war with an economy vastly expanded and technologically advanced.

Eric: I can guess what answer you would give but what was the government and media response to Russia's big educational advance? What evidence is there?

Ray: Briefly, the Robbins Report on Higher Education. Only one answer could be found to Russia's massive investment in a broad-based educational system leading to a pinnacle of technological excellence. The political will in the West was lacking until then, but the response by the British, as with the American Government, was an immediate and crash programme of expansion in technical and higher education from which the teaching profession benefitted. Apart from very welcome salary increases there were other effects. Before the contract for the college tennis courts was completed, plans were agreed for extending the building in their place. However, the contractors evidently had to be allowed to complete the tennis courts, so the day they were so beautifully finished the bulldozers came in and ripped them up and a large extension built.

Eric: What were you and the Communist Party of Great Britain doing at that time?

Ray: I remember discussing the drafts of resolutions for the Union Conference, especially the controversial ones on peace, disarmament and the redeployment of resources from 'defence' into education and health. Across the other side of the county I had long discussions with a like-minded Jack Tyrell who was influential in both the Union and CP, benefiting from his insights in the policies and actions that the right wing were already planning and countering - and they had the press and money at their disposal. It wasn't a question of smoke-filled rooms and secret deliberations and instructions, but the Communist Party had 'aggregate' meetings of members which enabled the leadership to know what was happening at grassroots level and enabled individuals to benefit from the overall picture and to word resolutions appropriately to have the maximum chance of success.

Eric: What was being printed in the mass newspapers about left organisations?

Ray: The newspapers and radio reflected the policies of the establishment, continually referring to subversion and 'entryism' by 'alien' political groups especially into the Labour Party and trades unions. This may have occurred with certain sectarian and ultra-left individuals, but my experience was the exact opposite. The Party devoted time, resources and energy that strengthened the union and the interests of its members with no direct benefit to itself. Indeed, my union work was escalating at the expense of the political and peace campaigning and later, when I moved to Scotland, I reversed these priorities. Blacklisting by employers via the Primrose League and MI5 went unchecked and an outstanding fellow member of the Communist Party, Eric Atkinson, has detailed how he was unjustifiably dispossessed of his livelihood by such means. The actions of MI5 spies in CND and the CPGB have been exposed by whistleblowers like Clive Ponting, David Shaylor and especially Kathleen Massiter who was imprisoned because she could no longer tolerate the misuse of the secret services to support the conservative policies of the Government. For example, in 1983 Thatcher gave Heseltine the task of campaigning against CND and exposing communist influence in it. Amusingly, it backfired when his spies reported that instead of communists influencing CND policy it was CND that was influencing Communist Party policy. Until the

Nineties I was refused a visa by the United States but I had the satisfaction of embarrassing the officials of the then US Consulate in Edinburgh when I discussed it with them. It is interesting that now, in the Nineties, the Data Protection Registrar, Elizabeth France, has asked MI5 to ensure that its files on over one million British citizens are accurate, relevant and up to date but MI5 have refused to involve any Government watchdog, so who knows what happens behind the cloak of unnecessary secrecy? As Jimmy Reid has described (*Scotsman*, August 29th, 1997), 'Historically and currently, British security services have equated defence of the realm with defence of the political *status quo*. Those who challenged or wanted to change that *status quo* were considered subversives or traitors; often accused of being agents of a foreign power. The real traitors (such as Blunt, Burgess, McLean, Philby and Cairncross) were considered sacrosanct because they had the right public school accents and contacts... The national security of Britain was thereby nearly strangled to death by the old school tie.' In reality, therefore, the traitors were found on the playing fields of Eton and in the ivory towers of Oxbridge; never in the Communist Party of Great Britain. Just read *"Spies, Lies and Whistleblowers"* (Book Guild 2005) by former MI5 officer, Annie Machon!

Eric: Aren't you trying to be too analytical and rational about human affairs when it's really about the majority of people being driven by their emotional drives?

Ray: Yes, I tend to agree. Everybody tries to rationalise what they do in order to justify their actions, but it seemed to me that the role of irrationalism in human affairs is not only exceedingly powerful but detrimental to the interests of others, and therefore, in the longer term, to oneself. If animals don't do the right thing they don't survive, so they tune in very sensitively to the real world around them. Hopefully we have gone beyond the mere survival of the fittest. Biologically humans are animals, but they are qualitatively different in their level of sophistication to the extent that they have the capacity to delude themselves as they struggle to match their emotional and intellectual responses. Why could this be?

Briefly, I would summarise it like this. The lower parts of the brain are programmed at birth, so that we can operate on automatic for much of the time. However, the higher parts involve a learning process, becoming actively engaged in making billions of interconnections in the construction of a very complex model of the world, as referred to in chapter one. This model acts as a frame of reference for subsequent input via the sense receptors leading to action or to its internalisation, which we call thinking and imagining. Humans do this consciously but this often comes into conflict with our baser instinctive feelings of fear, lust, envy, passion, greed, aggression and so on. How often, then, does our intellect accept something that our 'heart' doesn't, and vice-versa? The problem for me was how to accommodate this conflict of what I thought to be the necessary course of action propelled by long-term global considerations of changing society to work in the interests of the majority rather than a rich and powerful minority, as against my short-term interest in day-to-day family duties and pleasures and the inevitable conflicts of loyalty that this poses.

Eric: Why have you got such antagonism against the rich in society? They have surely earned their wealth and we could join them if we strove to do so? Where does the irrational come into the "haves and the have-nots"?

Ray: I am not talking about different rewards for work done. There is an increasing gap between the very rich and the very poor. Those with wealth, often inherited, are not only rich but form powerful élites deliberately perpetuating their positions by the exploitation of the irrational to the extent that religion, magic, superstition, legend, myths, cults and mystical philosophies have been used to retard human progress. On the other hand, these aspects of the human condition have always been with us and therefore must be part of a human need and even the most intelligent have been drawn to a belief in the supernatural. Having turned it over in my mind I concluded that, for instance, people need religion and other illusions as a solace in an unkind world, as an answer to the interminable questions that arise every day. It doesn't follow, however, that it's true. It may also be a fact that it makes law and order easier to maintain, just as Moses had to say to his unruly followers when he came down from the mountain with the commandments in tablets of stone that it was God who had given them to him. Life is much easier if we can invoke a higher authority, which makes the road to democracy so difficult to achieve, let alone the class struggle and the road to Socialism.

Eric: May I turn to your last remark and say that the electorate doesn't seem very interested in the road to socialism so you can't expect the candidates to put it into their manifestos. After all they have got to convince the voters about immediate concerns.

Ray: My experience seems to suggest that those interested in furthering their own interests in politics, with status, recognition, power, a career and future prospects have to pander to the lowest common denominator, be charming to their colleagues, the electorate and especially the media. In our type of confrontational democracy they also have to engage in slinging as much mud as possible at the opposition and to devise enough gimmickry to gain attention. In contrast, long and detailed discussions and debates of policies were certainly the order of the day in the Communist Party because this was no ladder of opportunity for the careerist politician but only for those interested in a commitment to a struggle on behalf of the disadvantaged majority of the population.

Eric: So you really thought that you were making progress by engaging in the so-called "battle of ideas"?

Ray: As one of my esteemed colleagues in Aberdeen, Annie Inglis, was later to remark, with the appropriate amount of academic cynicism, I seemed to have got the knack of campaigning for lost causes! Actually, it was a case of 'win some lose some' but however many 'battles' we lost we were sure we would win the 'war'. We told each other that history was with us. We believed in 'progress' and the ability of man to decide his own future, but for this we had to study the jungle warfare of capitalism in order to change society to a more just, fair and peaceful one, and in changing the world for the better we changed ourselves for the better. As the Chinese would say, the longest journey starts with a few steps. Because of the prevailing propaganda many connect the Communist Party of Great Britain with the Soviet Union. However, thinking globally and long term starts with thinking locally and short term, and the British Communist Party throughout its life can be credited with an enormous contribution to the advance of the Labour and Trades Union movements. Inasmuch as I was a small cog in this big wheel I am a happy man. With a tinge of nostalgia I can recall the donkey work, making placards, preparing meetings, selling the *Daily Worker*, door-to-door canvassing, fly-posting, telephoning, collecting money, travelling to demos and conferences and sitting through committee meetings in 'smoke-filled' rooms despite the hind sight and reflections as time elapsed.

TAPE SIX: LOCAL IS POLITICAL

Eric: Let's discuss your move to Scotland and your opinions then as an 'incomer' adopting a new identity. In September 1997 Steven Bayley wrote in the New Statesman:-

"National identity is a delicate and precarious mixture of shared symbols, happy accidents, evolutionary chaos, historical inheritance, genetic roulette, political interference, cultural hand-me-downs, economics, the weather, geology, sunspots, Iron Age migration patterns, religion, bus routes, taste, landscape, the Gulf Stream and investment decisions made in Delaware or Zurich." Did you feel any of this when you crossed the border?

Ray: Moving from the leafy suburbs of Greater London to the centre of Aberdeen, the Granite City some five hundred and fifty miles to the North, marked a sea change in our physical and cultural environment that looked more like emigrating than moving. However, we knew that there were plenty of jobs that we could go back to if necessary, and the children were at their most moveable age, so mobility wasn't a problem. We didn't feel as though we were burning our boats. The Sixties is marked down in most people's minds as the decade of change with a youth culture, a sexual revolution and the flowering of ideas in fashion and lifestyles. For me, it was a decade of intense political involvement, of family life and my assimilation into another nation.Our image of Scotland in general, and that of Aberdeen in particular, had been coloured by the media, although I knew something about its geography. Mary and I had also been on holiday on the West Coast, but separately as this was before we had actually met. We were typically English in our estimations of it - mountains and lochs, shipyards and coal, sheep and fish, bagpipes and haggis, Hogmanay and heather, ceilidhs and whisky - the familiar montage that still remains as the image of Scotland in so many people's minds today. I had also met some people from Scotland at sea, in political conferences and in education, but I knew better than to generalise from the characteristics of people away from home, especially 'ex-pats'.At my first school in Middlesex, Ruislip Manor, the art teacher was a Mr Simpson, who never seemed to have enough money on a Friday to pay for the week's tea money in the staff room, but I never supported my colleagues' remarks that 'All Scotsmen are mean...' For Aberdeen, in particular, there are numerous jokes, like the Aberdeen taxi that crashed and twenty-two passengers got out unhurt! Aberdeen also has the reputation of being parochial, and indeed it was until the oil boom made it a cosmopolitan city. The local paper, the *Aberdeen Press and Journal* that has a bigger local circulation than all the other newspapers put together, still regards international news with some ambivalence. At the time of the sinking of the *Titanic* the headline on the front page was 'Aberdeen man drowned at sea!

Eric: But these differences seem rather superficial. Were there any of significance?

Ray: When I sat through national conferences and meetings in England I thought that the Scots made the best contributions, and reflected a more advanced political culture than the one in which I had cut my teeth. I was thirty-five and at the height of my capabilities, not so much ambitious as intensely forward-looking, whether domestically, professionally or politically. I was amused by the local accent and the 'Doric', a north-east dialect with 'loons and quines' (lads and lassies), 'yer ken' (you know), 'fit like?' (how are you?), 'puddocks and horny gollocks' (frogs and earwigs) and a thousand others. I was also being made aware of a different sense of community and culture, stemming from a different history. The different legal system was obvious as soon as we negotiated the purchase of our house in Great Western Road. In England, either party can withdraw from the sale until written contracts have been exchanged and signed, and we were let down by the first buyer and had to put the house up for sale again. Meanwhile, in Scotland, a verbal agreement is a contract so we had two houses for a brief spell! Of all the hundreds of differences in the law, I think the vast majority are better in Scotland, particularly because they are based on the 'good of the community' rather than the property rights of the aristocracy as in England. What I immediately liked about Scotland was its variety, not just of landscape but of people. You quoted from the New Statesman. In the previous edition, Brian Groom describes the Scots as 'So talented yet so truculent, so adventurous yet so parochial. So vociferous yet so strangely compliant.' I would sum it up more succinctly as unity in diversity.

Eric: Did you know anything about Scottish Education before went for interview?

Ray: I swatted up the details of the different educational system I was now to engage in, but I had underestimated the implications. At least I had found an intelligible system, as against the absence of an overall system in England.

Eric: Let me stop you there. What of the broader cultural differences from England?

One of the biggest cultural differences was one that is still wrongly perceived in England - that of national aspirations. So often is it portrayed as national chauvinism, or more critically as the 'whingeing Scots' when, at base, it is a question of democracy and the right of all peoples to have a say in deciding their own future rather than having this imposed against their will. People in England would only understand this burning frustration if the Westminster Parliament was dissolved and they were governed totally from Brussels! Here, in Scotland, we had a secretary of state, accountable only to the prime minister in London who appointed him, having the power to go roughshod over the opinions of the majority and imposing his own, heading a Scottish Office employing fifteen thousand with a budget of fifteen billion pounds, appointing over one hundred and sixty quangos and giving only five billion pounds to the local authorities over which he exercises his right to intervene and limit their activities. Hence the 'Claim of Right' and the movement for a Scottish Parliament, which was only later to develop a profile demanding the recognition it deserved, forcing a Labour Government to take action.One cannot overestimate the significance of devolution, obtained after years of campaigning, for a Parliament in Scotland radically different from that of Westminster. It involves proportional representation, a gender balance, normal working hours, committees with executive powers, consensual rather than a confrontational style of politics and weight given to the recommendations of non-governmental organisations. It is interesting that it was the Labour Party that insisted on the Additional Member System of PR with a list system that gave them the power to rank the candidates, instead of the Single Tranferable Vote which would give that power to the electorate, but, in turn, led to the more sophisticated electorate giving their second vote instead to minority parties like the Socialists and Greens!

Eric: Can you give me an example of what was actually happening on the ground? It was Harold Wilson who said that a week in politics is a long time, but it seems to me that the converse is also true. The development of an idea whose time has come sometimes takes a long time to incubate, filter through the population and get acted on by the decision-makers. Hence the role of civic society and its organisations and the activists who campaign on their behalf. I therefore look back to the sixties' in the Aberdeen Peace Council, Peace Festivals and especially in the Committee for Peace in Vietnam with its lobbies to Parliament, demonstrations, letter writing, fund-raising for medical aid and ceaseless work in committees.

Eric: One of the world shaking events of the sixties was the Cuban missile crisis. Comentators were speculating on World War 3 but how did you react to it?

Ray: Shortly after my arrival in Aberdeen the Cuban crisis broke out and the threat of nuclear war between the superpowers was very real. The United States could no longer rule Cuba by proxy in order to further its economic and political interests. Fidel Castro nationalised the sugar industry and aimed at getting resources redeployed into health and education in order to relieve the abject poverty, especially in the rural areas. America blockaded but failed in several attempts to overthrow Castro's government. The U.S. declared that Cuba lay in its sphere of influence and therefore had no right to nationalise American companies. At this time Castro was not a communist, but he was forced to trade and get help from the Soviet Union, with agreements to exchange sugar for oil and military support to defend himself. In 1962 America declared a total blockade of Cuba as a Russian convoy was crossing the Atlantic and missiles were identified on the decks of some of the ships. Kruschev declared that the missiles were to defend Cuba's sovereignty and that America's action was illegal under international law. The ships were not armed and must be allowed passage in international waters. American warships went to intercept the convoy and halt its passage by any means available and the Russians insisted that the ships were to proceed to Cuba. A clash on the high seas would quickly escalate into nuclear confrontation. The American submarines and the supply ship left the Holy Loch. The British armed services were put on full alert. The convoy was approaching the ring of American warships. I joined the biggest and most representative protest march that Aberdeen had ever seen, with a flood of banners along Union Street urging, 'Hands off Cuba'.

Eric: I remember the end of the confrontation but what led to it?

Ray: I wrote to my MP, hoping the letter would arrive in time. The confrontation was timed for three o'clock in the afternoon of what I seem to recollect as a Tuesday. The day was calm and sunny, yet a thick gloom pervaded everything and everybody, including the media. Suddenly it was announced that the convoy had turned back and was heading for the Black Sea ports from whence it came. The headlines declared that the Soviet Union had been defeated by calling its bluff. America showed itself to be invincible. Castro would fall - as the press has been predicting for the last half century. The agreement between Kennedy and Kruschev was that Russian missiles would be withdrawn from Cuba immediately and America would not invade. This in itself was all that Russia and Cuba wanted, but, in order that Kennedy got domestic support not to invade Cuba, Russia had also agreed to keep secret the American agreement to remove its missiles from the Turkish border which threatened the Soviet Union. This was projected as a defeat for Russia by all the media rejecting reports of the deal. That is, except the *Morning Star* whose readers were the only one privileged with the truth as on so many other occasions. Now, over forty years later, Geoffrey Hodgson who was then Washington correspondent of the *Observer* is able to reveal in the *New Stateman* (24-10-97) that 'With cheerful ruthlessness Kennedy leaked that it was only Adlai Stevenson - his defeated rival for the Democratic nomination - who had wanted a deal. Henceforth, any suggestion that there had been one could be dismissed as the ravings of the soft-on-communism left. I have found that it is this type of manipulation of any by the media that is one of the most potent causes of the cynicism permeating today's electorate. Locally, one result of the Cuban crisis was a wider list of contacts and support for CND and the Peace Council. I therefore quickly got to know who were the main defenders in Aberdeen of these issues of world peace. I also found that communists played a leading role in the unions and the peace movement as well as in their own highly respected party organisation.

Eric: That's all very well but I'm itching to hear of what was actually happening inside the communist party at that time. What were your personal experiences as you saw them?

Ray: The day I arrived in Aberdeen I went to introduce myself to the area secretary, whose address I had previously obtained in order to get some general contextual information about the political scene. I met Margaret Rose at Maberly House, near the centre and a stone's throw from the college. She was very hospitable, enthusiastic and knowledgeable, running her house as a working men's hostel and with an office and meeting room in a large shed at the back, well-known as the party headquarters for north-east Scotland with its four hundred members. There were about a dozen branches, some industrial like the transport (buses) and rails branches, others based on the locality such as the election wards of Mastrick and Northfields. All the information was at Maberly House. A handful of members did not want their identity disseminated, but there were no 'open' and 'closed' lists as I remember hearing about before the war. There was always the possibility of MI5 infiltration and this occurred at higher levels; for many years the London office was bugged, until it was discovered during redecoration. It was never a problem except on tactical grounds as our attitude was that if anyone joined and made a contribution in energy or finance he or she would be very welcome. I was elected membership secretary. We were never engaged in any other than legitimate political campaigning but certain members had to have their anonymity respected in order to avoid threats to their livelihood. Whether or not people agreed with the politics, the Communist Party and individual members were well respected locally, despite the terrible lies, innuendoes and attacks nationally by all the media. I remember a colleague with whom I engaged in quite serious discussion during coffee and lunch breaks. He approached me with a different question every day and sympathised with the answers. He then asked me if I was a member of the Labour Party, one of the many Trotskyite groups, and continued down a list. He then said I should join something instead of keeping my ideas to myself, to which I finally told him I was in the Communist Party. 'Anything but that! What are people going to think of me if they see me talking to you?' and we never held a conversation again. Such was the guilt by association that the establishment cultivated with respect to the CPGB, but, of course, from their point of view it was the only real challenge to the perpetuation of their privilege and power.

Eric: Apart from your political role who were the comrades you were working with?

Ray: My privilege was being associated with so many outstanding human beings devoted to the betterment of others less fortunate, such as Bob Cooney of the International Brigade in Spain, John Bacon, a scientist, May Balnaves, a lecturer in English, Jimmy Oats, teacher and union man, Jimmy Milne, who became one of the best general secretaries of the STUC, Bill Henderson, painter and decorator, always an excellent candidate in the Council elections, Andy Smith and the campaign against joining the Common Market, Sid English, the Lennox family, the Thomson family and Norrie Williamson, who accompanied me countless times selling the *Morning Star* and who died suddenly of a heart attack after standing for many hours collecting for medical aid for Vietnam on a cold, wet and windy Saturday in Union Street. It would be boring to add to the list, but there were many many others beavering away at a local level, without any reward for themselves save the satisfaction of tackling injustice, poverty, ignorance and the misery inflicted by the jungle warfare of capitalism where the devil takes the hindmost. There were, of course, those who chose to leave the Party and advance themselves as they could not do by remaining inside, but who can blame them?The social side was also well developed, with many of the Scottish traditional singing, dancing and drinking sessions, but I didn't take part and I was thought of as a bit of a loner and even unsociable, but I was keen to return home and to Mary and the children, as I knew they didn't appreciate my frequent absences. I looked on the Party as being more important than my pleasures and welfare, but others may have thought that this subservience to 'good causes' should only come a long way down my list of activities after my wife and the family.

Eric: I know that party machines don't like to wash their linen in public but I heard that you had a personality clash with the secretary. How did that arise?

Ray: There was one particular episode in the annals of the Party history of Aberdeen which I felt it to be my unpleasant duty to act upon. The area secretary, Margaret Rose, had no more diligent assistant than myself. She was a tireless worker too. We drafted leaflets, bulletins, news sheets and letters, replicating them on the Gestetner. I was instrumental in drafting and distributing a powerful one on comprehensive education which was widely distributed. Material for meetings of the branch and area was prepared, including proposals for action that had been decided at the Scottish Committee. Democratic centralism was the key principle underlying the work and organisation of the Party, whereby discussions on all issues were discussed at all levels, representatives were elected to the next level in the hierarchy and decisions at a higher level subsumed those at a lower one. In theory it was democratic. Every member could say what they wanted to say and they did. It was centralist inasmuch as decisions on policy and action were handed down in order to get things done in a unified and concerted manner as effectively as possible. The Party was not a talking shop.Margaret Rose was a powerful character, and her goal was to get policy implemented as quickly as possible, but she became intolerant of those who didn't see things her way. A few years passed and I became uneasy at her unwarranted criticism and even condemnation of those with whom she did not see eye to eye. An increasing number of members avoided her, and at first I defended her as the key worker, volunteering to do all the day-to-day work. Finally, I put the situation in front of her. She not only insisted on the opposite but her ego trips were extended, and I wrote a long and detailed letter to Gordon McLennan, then Scottish Secretary, proposing her removal and, in order not to be accused of going behind her back I sent her a copy. The storm that followed led to her eventual resignation but then had no use of her premises. With the help of loans from two other comrades I bought, on behalf of the Party, a shop at 21 Urquhart Road, and a group of us furnished and equipped it and reinvigorated the membership at a time of difficult political circumstances, but in our view action was no less urgent.

Eric How did you cope at the time when the cold war deepened quite alarmingly?

Ray: To the outside world who listened to the continuous anti-communist propaganda we were mere agents of Moscow. For a long time differences with the CPSU were not expressed outside the Party as that would have given fuel to the non-stop crusade against us by blowing up stories of splits and dissent and causing disarray in the party. Actually, as long ago as the 1951 *British Road to Socialism* spelt out the parliamentary road to socialism replacing 'the crises, insecurity, profiteering, inequalities and social antagonisms of capitalist society'. The differing views of the British delegation to the 1964 International Conference of Communist Parties were accepted as valid points of view by the CPSU. The CPGB was particularly concerned at the action taken against dissidents and questions of inner party democracy in the Soviet Union, but we accepted the leading role played by the Soviet Union as the only way to defend socialism.

Eric: Did you meet anyone from the Soviet Union at that time and get their views?

Ray: Soviet ships regularly visited Aberdeen from Murmansk to unload timber. Occasionally, some of us visited them, were shown around and chatted to whoever spoke some English. They could go ashore but had no convertible currency to buy sterling so they could only window-shop, unlike the Polish crews who would be seen buying for their home market. The morning after a casual visit to a Soviet ship, there was a phone call from the captain stating that one of their sailors had not returned the previous evening and that the police had denied any knowledge of his whereabouts. We went down to the ship, phoned the police HQ and got nowhere. To cut a long story short, the sailor was brought back four days later by the police and dropped off at the foot of the gangway. He was an eighteen year old on his first voyage, had lost his way back to ship, knew no English and had stopped a police car. Having been indoctrinated to think that 'Russians want to escape', they took him to Craiginches Prison for interview, but it was a bank holiday weekend in England and the Home Office Russian-speaking official was not available. There was, of course, a Russian department at the university, and also teachers of Russian in the schools, but the police had instructions to deny everything until the Home Office had dealt with it. Yet, in Britain, we are supposed to know who the police are holding.

Eric: One swallow doesn't make a summer! That occasion was surely an exception to the rule of British law? But let's move on.

Ray: I don't want to exaggerate as previous generations have achieved a lot with hard struggle I might add but another such denial of human rights occurred when a well-known Irish psychiatrist, whom I heard speak about the denial of the right to work, council houses and jobs to Catholics in Derry. This was before 'Bloody Sunday', when British troops fired and killed over a dozen of them in a peaceful demonstration. She was arrested on suspicion of harbouring an IRA suspect in her large house in the Midlands where she was well-known for giving hospitality. All her activities were open for anyone to see. She was publicly critical of the IRA and emphasised the political way forward as the only one to take. When I heard on the radio about her arrest I was taken aback and wrote to all I could. I supported the campaign for her release as she was being kept indefinitely in prison without charge. After several months she was released, but her job had been given to someone else and her private life was devastated. Ninety-two per cent of the 7,397 people held under the Prevention of Terrorism Act between 1972 and 1992 were never charged, and many who were charged were released after many years when their innocence was finally proved. How many more examples of miscarriages of justice have I got to give, even from my limited experience, before we question the closed nature of our society - the 'Free World'?

Eric: What did you think of the dissidents in the Soviet Union which I can tell you about because they have always been given great publicity?

Ray: I completely agree that the injustices of capitalism don't make the injustices under socialist regimes excusable. At first, we called it 'enemy propaganda'. Then it was the 'growing pains' of a new system under threat. I tended to say that it was a continuation of the previous regime's well-tried methods that were part of the culture, but I heard no one in the communist party defend Stalin's crimes. These revelations were a shock to us all but they were nothing to do with socialism. Some comrades left the Communist Party, viewing human nature in more glowing terms than others, including myself, who tried to differentiate between what the present situation was, a complex mixture of the good and the bad, and what we wanted it to be. Stalin's daughter Svetlana wrote a book of her life in 1967 describing life and death around her and then emigrated to America. In 1984 she reflected on how her views had changed. She said, "I think every Soviet defector feels the same way the moment he gets out. You greatly exaggerate all the freedoms, you idealise the free world; in my generation that meant you were idealising America above everything. In the beginning you are in a kind of ecstasy and euphoria. Later on you learn what the reality is and it is in many ways a disappointment... What I did not realise 17 years ago was how similar the two superpowers are, both in good ways and bad. Now I see two nuclear powers whose ideas about each other are based on totally obsolete propaganda, on the concepts of 40 years ago. It upsets me and frightens me and it is a question of politics, not people.... Yes, many terrible things have happened in the Soviet Union, but so they have to some degree or other in most parts of the world. The thing about the Gulag is that it has been overblown. I don't mean at that it was not true - it was all true - but since

Solzhenitsyn people think there is nothing else in Soviet Russia. I feel that Solzhenitsyn has brought more hatred into the world than understanding. After all, the USSR is also a society where millions of people have got free education, the chance of going to university, and free medical care. You cannot deny that this has been an improvement for them. And how come we have all these chess-players and dancers and musicians, astronauts and scientists and sportsmen? And how was it that millions of Soviet citizens fought for their country in a war and did not turn against it?"

Eric: So what Svetlana heard and read when she fled to the West was the negative and never the positive about the Soviet Union. But why didn't the CPGB criticise its policies?

Ray: In simple terms we tried to balance the picture that people had, but, of course, we were also reluctant to criticise the Soviet Union in public However, a shake-out began after Hungary in 1956, and especially after our open disagreement with the CPSU over Czechoslovakia in 1968. The *Morning Star*, reflecting the views of the Executive Committee of the CPGB, became ever more publicly critical of the CPSU and this led to the hijacking of the paper by its editorial staff and breakaways from the Party such as the New Communist and Party Communist Party of Britain. It was downhill after that. I kept to the mainstream and was loyal to the end but never uncritical. I don't think there is a contradiction there. It just seemed to me that the political situation always demanded a movement that campaigned on the key issues of the moment. The Communist Party was the most effective organisation trying to do this, if it could avoid the dogmatism and sectarianism that had been self-defeating in the past. Also it had to avoid the revisionism and reformism that had led all Labour organisations to end up trying to make capitalism work better than the Tories, with the inevitable consequence of furthering the interests of the wealthy lest they move their capital abroad. Now in 2010 the Inland Revenue say that £90 billion in tax have been lost in Britain since the financial crisis of 2008 by tax avoidance schemes by wealthy individuals and multinationals like Amazon, Google, Starbucks and several others. This, in turn, meant reducing public expenditure and making the poor poorer. The 'trickle down' theory, whereby the wealthy would be able to spend even more, pushing up employment, was given as a justification but has never been shown to work in practice.

Eric: I'd like to return to the topic of the Soviet Union.You made several visits didn't you?

Ray: The post of lecturer in geography was to start on April 1st, 1962, but I had already organised an educational tour to Warsaw and Moscow for the Easter holidays, having circulated union members in Surrey. There were over forty applications and although it was tailor-made for us it was organised through Progressive Tours, the only company with tours to the Soviet Union. Passing from West to East Germany was more tedious, but Progressive Tours had already sent the passenger list for visas so I found a welcoming official and I gave the names of our absentees. The train had then to pass through a West German station, but it was not a scheduled stop. At a time when all references to the Eastern bloc were tarred with the same brush, it surprised people to see such contrasts between and within the different countries there. In Poland, the guard and officials were in a compartment at the end of the carriage drinking vodka. In the Soviet Union, the carriages and dining car were continually being cleaned and 'stakhans' of tea brought round. The farming landscape changed radically from East Germany's collective farms and tractors to Poland's smallholdings and horsedrawn ploughs and then back to the large fields, lakes and forests of Byelorussia. We spent a day in schools and sightseeing in Warsaw which I had intended as a break from the long journey, but it was enough to get people talking about it for some time after. The real objective was Moscow and I subsequently wrote articles about the educational system as I saw it. I started by explaining that it was not so much communist as continental, that the ingredients were a mixture of history, ideology, and pragmatism.

Eric: No doubt the report you made to the Teacher's Union was glowing with optimism?

Ray: It would be easy to say now that my glasses were rose-tinted, but I was also conscious that there had to be a countervailing influence against the unremitting attacks on all aspects of Soviet life which imbued most of the population of the West with a very warped and, indeed, demonstrably outrageous view of the facts. It was certainly the case that although everything was new to me it wasn't *news* to me. I was not taken by surprise and shaken abruptly as some of my colleagues were, who had to change some of their cherished opinions while at the same time using the 'exceptions' clause, 'We were only shown the best...', in order to try to accommodate the incongruities between what they had read and what they had experienced. In other words, who had been previously brainwashed, me or them?

Eric: I notice that you have an Aberdeen M.Ed. What was your particular interest or thesis?

Ray: One of the findings of my study was the crucial importance of the headteacher in accounting for the differences in staying on. For example, Bill Christie at Summerhill Junior Secondary had introduced certificate courses and ran a variety of after-school activities, with a much bigger proportion staying on than at Northfield, which had a similar socio-economic catchment area. As a matter of interest, Christie was followed by R.F. Mackenzie from Braehead in Fife, and he turned the school into quite a different direction, with its main emphasis on education for leisure and making school a much more attractive place for the less able. R.F. Mackenzie stated in his subsequent book, *The Unbowed Head*, that society as organised at present is a jungle. 'It has clearings of caring people here and there, but the pattern isn't one of caring. We are entering the dark days,' he insisted. 'The "Ode to Joy" is postponed.' He said it was essential to change society by starting with the young citizens of tomorrow as the only hope for the future. In my opinion he seemed to have forgotten that the whole of the educational system is devised to perpetuate the present society and its needs. Parents and employers were looking to the employment prospects of school leavers. This radical change of emphasis from academic work to leisure activities divided the staff, led to public debate and accusations and eventually to his suspension and dismissal. I had the opportunity to discuss some of his ideas with him as a visiting lecturer from the college. I admired his caring attitude for the generally neglected majority of our children, but I had also admired Christie's determination to give as many as possible a chance to climb the educational ladder, and the way he went out and about the corridors, classrooms and playground, meeting and encouraging students and staff rather than staying in his room and administering from a distance. Both factions denied that there could be two different approaches operating in the same school, but that was before comprehensive education was implemented to do just that.

Eric: Ah! that's what I want to ask you about - the "before" and "after" situation. Was there a real difference in the educational world with comprehensive schools? Comprehensive education is not surely a panacea for the social ills of society?

Ray: Labour Party friends were keen to defeat the proposals, and at a public meeting to announce his half-baked proposals I laid bare the tactics the Chief Education Officer was using now that he realised that the *status quo* was untenable. He was visibly taken aback, and the hall reverberated with muffled murmurings and the turning of heads. The chairman rapidly moved on to the next question.I doubt whether I should have been so outspoken, especially when I similarly opposed what the college principal had said at a big conference on the topic, even though I took the precaution of not mentioning him personally. I had also organised a letter to the *Press and Journal* signed by about thirty of the lecturing staff, declaring that the *status quo* was no longer serving us well and proposing the comprehensive alternative. It appeared on the front page and annoyed the principal, even though we had signed in our personal capacities.My colleague, May

Balnaves who was also in the CPGB, told me how I was jeopardising my prospects for promotion and later a friend on the governing body brought up the question of my discrimination after hearing the principal's remarks that my politics made me unsuitable for a post of higher responsibility. I think it was ironic therefore that some years later, when the opportunity again arose, no voices were raised in a similar manner. I say 'ironic' because had there been genuine objections to my promotion they may have been suspected of being a cover for unacceptable political objections! Of course, I think that I had been worthy of promotion the first time round! More importantly, Aberdeen went ahead with a fully comprehensive system from eleven to eighteen.

Eric: You haven't told me anything about your career. For most men this has been their major concern, certainly in terms of the time and energy they put into it. Was yours worthwhile enough to tell me about it?

Ray: Of course it was a major part of my life and immensely worthwhile and interesting. I have felt and seen the positive results of my academic career, although I accept that all teachers give themselves credit for their successes and ascribe other reasons for their failures. But I feel that this is not the main issue here. My professional life has been successful but repeated by thousands of others. It was only a contributory factor in the making of 'a left-wing activist'- contributory inasmuch as it was background to my interest, knowledge and commitment to global problems, and was reflected in the need for local action.

Eric: Well then, comment on how your personal relationships affected your political engagement. Remember that the title is A Political Dialogue.

Ray: Similar in a way to my professional life, my home and family life, ongoing and changing as it has been, is significant here to the extent it has both helped and hindered my conviction that individuals have got to stand up and be counted. As I was convinced that something had to be done about the movement to defend the interests of the vast majority against the unrelenting downward pressure from a rich, greedy and power-hungry minority I found it hard but satisfying. Because it was an intellectual conviction rather than a psychological need for me to be involved, I had to pressure myself to take action. This might even seem absurd to those who have labelled me as a 'doer' rather than a 'thinker'. It helps to have the capacity for hard work, the health to carry on for long periods, the determination to see things through to the end, but I drove myself from conviction, sometimes against what I would have liked to have done for short-term advantage, and therefore it was always just as easy to relax, change activity, move on or do nothing, like the chap who just sat and thought, and sometimes just sat!

Eric: Why not do one's bit and leave others to do the rest as it seems easy to 'burn-out?

Ray: Yes, it is always so easy to take the line of least resistance, and it may, unfortunately, be the case that each generation has to learn afresh the problems of living together and how to respond to them. A sophisticated education may help the individual to contribute to the collective conscience, but one cannot be optimistic that human misery can be removed on the time-scale that is necessary. It may well be that catastrophes, not too small to be ignored and not too big as to be overwhelming, will have to occur before whole peoples are galvanised into action. It seemed to me that my biggest problem was not myself, although we all have a habit of deluding ourselves when it is convenient to do so, but rather persuading those who professed that they wanted change to move themselves out of their armchairs. My approach was to persuade if I could, compromise if I must and leave alone if they opposed. In my attempts to get some commitment and action, those with families who were often convinced but 'had neither time nor money' I sympathised with, but older people seemed to have, in my humble opinion, a disproportionate say in the decision-making process. I therefore resolved not to make excuses on my own behalf in order to lighten my load Young people were more in evidence voicing their political opinions in the Sixties and Seventies than in the remaining part of the century, but they tended to move on to other locations, interests and jobs. Yet their enthusiasm and creative abilities were not only welcome but seen as the basis of the future of any movement or organisation and therefore had to be given support wherever possible. It also meant the occasional paying of their debts as occurred when the YCL booked a hall and a film projector but was unable to pay the bill. Through necessity I had compartmentalised my life as I played the different roles of a political organiser in the Party and as secretary for many years of the Committee for Peace in Vietnam and the Aberdeen Peace Council, as lecturer in geography and especially that of father and husband.

Eric: What about the Sixties as an historical period with, of course, the benefit of hindsight?

Ray: The Sixties have become known historically for the sexual revolution that is supposed to have occurred. There was no doubt that a teenage culture was in full flow. Young people had buying power. Consumer goods were now being produced in abundance and they needed markets. Advertisers seized on this easy marketing of such things as fashion clothes, records, Coke and entertainment. Young people worked or got reasonable student grants. The dating game was more obvious and premarital sex was unashamedly discussed. Students particularly engaged in social and political issues, and took part in demonstrations on apartheid, women's lib, Rhodesia and especially Vietnam. Unlike today's students, who feel insecure and worried about their job prospects, those who qualified found work. They had the luxury to think of the world outside and the ability to question events around them. The traditional roles of men and women were changing, but why hadn't this happened earlier? Philip Larkin, the poet, said that sexual intercourse began in 1963, meaning, of course, that nobody talked frankly about it until then. In fact, the word 'teenager' was only in current usage after Elvis Presley's number one hit 'Rock Around The Clock' in the late Fifties, being imported into Britain soon after. Demographically, the post-war baby boom became a teenage boom in the Sixties, so that there were more than a few different aspects giving young people prominence. Much has been written about the Sixties - as though they registered a turning point in the evolution of British culture and politics. Was society disintegrating or was the deadwood of unwanted tradition being cut away? Were people more optimistic or pessimistic about the future? Did 'freedom' at last break out, with the casting aside of moral codes? What about The Beatles and the guitar-rich pop group culture? What about Carnaby Street and a new consumerism countered by flower-power and opting out? Was there a recognition of a more pluralistic society and the rise of feminism and environmentalism? Where was Prime Minister Wilson's cutting edge of a white-hot technological revolution? The redevelopment of many city centres, the pulling down of slum dwellings and the erection of concrete and glass tower blocks made visible a change in policy, ideas and particularly fashion. It seemed to me that it was probably a confused mix of different aspirations and also the result of the increased access to the immediacy of television, but I certainly caught hold of the change in attitudes from the wartime generation that 'made do', to a younger generation rejecting the prescriptions of their elders. It also seemed to me that Britain's role in the Cold War had a knock-on effect that led to a disillusionment and a cynicism that laid the basis for the advance of Thatcherism a decade later - but more momentous events happened to me meantime.

TAPE SEVEN: PEACE IS POLITICAL

Eric: We now come to a period of significant change especially at the international as well as the national level. Start with the Communist Party as you are the only witness I know who can tell it from his own experience.

Ray: I was campaigning mainly on local and peace issues but looking back it was perhaps more significant than we realised at the time due to the change in the fortunes of the Communist Party as it became openly Eurocommunist, and the pro-Soviet *Morning Star* divorced itself from it. Other factors to be taken into account were the end of the Vietnamese War and the general disillusionment with the Labour Government's implementation of right-wing policies and increasing confusion amongst the old and young people alike. At the time, all the signs were hopeful that the Left was gathering strength and I attended demonstrations in support of the UCS workers, who won their famous victory over closures, the successful miners strike of '74, and the students also took a leading role at protest meetings, vigils and marches for Peace in Vietnam. There were also militant movements in Europe and North America, so that we were optimistic in our view that socialist policies would eventually prevail - as these mass movements of ordinary people became politicised - and that the left within the Labour Party would eventually win the day. Gerry Hassan, a feature writer in the Scotsman has said, "The Communist Party was 'in the Labour movement but not the Labour Party, and in Scotland, with a small-sized Labour membership, the Communist Party had a disproportionate influence. This was famously evident in the Upper Clyde Shipbuilders (UCS) work-in of 1971-72, in its support for cross-party campaigns and in particular on home rule." which, of course, is now topping the news in Scotland. There were always strong debates within the meetings of the membership of the Communist Party, especially after 1956, but as I have said, no dirty washing was washed in public as the media would have used it to the exclusion of anything positive. However, following the 1968 Soviet Intervention in Czechoslovakia, the Party publicly condemned it, and this was followed by increasingly open criticism of the USSR, especially with regard to the arrest of dissidents. The dilemma was attempting a balance that would not merely add to the cold-war rhetoric of the West, but at the same time would let people know of our concerns. Many of us thought that to redress the balance it helped to support the events of the Scotland-USSR Society and its subsidiary Sovscot Tours, and to publicise the positive aspects of the Soviet experiment in the face of a vicious campaign to subvert it in every way. I well remember a remarkable and seminal speech by John Gollan on the problems of the International Communist movement not long before his untimely death.

Eric: How did that affect your vision of the future and especially about socialism?

Ray: As one grows older, uncertainties and problems increase, solutions are less obvious and urgent, whether or not these are personal or political. Of course, the contemplation of uncertainty is uniquely human, not shared by any other species. We have developed a consciousness of ourselves and the world that enables us to ponder the fragility of our existence and that of the lives of others, which, for the majority, is tragic and miserable. A countervailing evolutionary strategy is to allow our hormones to run, to live in the present and enjoy the moment of eating or mating, with the optimism of the struggle to parent our children and the concomitants of working, playing or merely surviving. An antidote to uncertainty and pessimism lies in religion and superstition or the assumption that science will provide the necessary technical fix that imbues American society. Fortunately younger people everywhere are filled with optimism. Unfortunately, they only learn slowly from history and it is questionable whether human beings will collectively learn quickly enough to cope with the massive problems confronting them.

Eric: I met you when you came to Edinburgh after your retirement. That must have been a big change in your activities after moving and taking a new job.

Ray: Only on the political activities. Not long after we moved to Edinburgh in 1984, I offered our help to the Miners' Welfare in Dalkeith during the famous Miners' Strike. We took food and jumble and met some outstanding characters in both the miners and their wives. There was a great feeling of camaraderie and solidarity, and support groups in Edinburgh were continually growing throughout the twelve months of the strike. I thought that Mick McGahey would have handled the strike better than

Arthur Scargill by a more subtle campaign against government policy, balloting members and forcing negotiations to acceptable solutions, but I have no doubt whatever about the sheer ruthlessness of the Thatcher Government in its diabolical objectives. Few people realised at the time that the Thatcher Government had planned for it during the previous years by building up stocks of coal, changing the power stations' fuel to oil, building gas-fired and nuclear-powered stations, bringing in laws restricting the activities of trades unions and stopping social security payments to the families of striking miners. The Government, in its aim to make the trades unions ineffective, knew that it had to defeat the miners 'no matter the cost', and spent one billion pounds in doing so.

Part of the attack was the involvement of the secret services, detailed in the hundreds of pages of Seumas Milne's 1994 book, *The Enemy Within*, stating that no effort nor expense was spared, 'from the secret financing of strike-breakers to mass electronic surveillance, from the manipulation of agents provocateurs to attempts to "fit-up" miners' officials, in order to discredit the union and its leaders. It is a record of the abuse of unaccountable power...' etc. Miners' wives, who had previously been passive observers, became active on their husbands' behalf. Many of them became politically literate and remarkably eloquent and I knew some of them who subsequently took education courses and interesting jobs, so that the legacy of the strike was not altogether negative.

Eric: You told me that you have been a member of the Campaign for Nuclear Disarmament since the Nineteen Fifties. Were you active in Edinburgh?

Ray: I think my activities in Edinburgh were particularly fruitful. I joined the local CND group in Stockbridge in 1984, which met in the primary school the first Monday evening of every month. It was a very flourishing campaigning group of two hundred with about forty active members. I joined a rota at the stall in the centre of Stockbridge every Saturday morning, selling badges and books, but also giving away leaflets and our current newsletter, as well as asking people to sign a petition or, indeed, to join us. Local and national demonstrations were well supported and our vertical banners made by Dick Sneddon became well known for their distinctiveness, as on the photo, montage on the front cover. In December our own Christmas card was distributed, inviting people to our carol singing under the council-erected illuminated tree, but my own interest lay in the problem of how to influence our decision-makers. I became the group's representative on the council's newly-formed Peace Forum.

In 1984 Thatcher was riding high as a consequence of the jingoism of the Falklands War, but in Edinburgh the long-standing Conservative majority was overturned by Labour. In 1985, the convenor of the Peace Forum, Councillor Dickie Alexander, proposed a Peace Weekend in the Assembly Rooms, George Street, for the beginning of March 1986. These prestigious premises belonged to the council and were administered by their recreation department and included different-sized rooms and halls readily available at this slack time of the year. I proposed that it should be a Peace Festival with a whole range of events for a wide variety of organisations, involving as many people as possible, with serious meetings, light entertainment, exhibitions and stalls, and a café and a bar all under the one roof. A small organising committee was formed, including myself, Alan Wilkie and John Doney from the Peace Forum, Roger Jones, deputy director of the recreation department, the manager of the Assembly Rooms and Councillor Alexander, with myself as the main co-ordinator. Its outstanding success led to an independent committee being elected, chaired by myself, with a grant from the council to organise a second one in 1987, which was almost too ambitious for the volunteers, who were experiencing this for the first time but, again, it was outstandingly successful, whatever criteria could be applied.

Eric: Were there any dissenting voices or problems you hadn't foreseen as you were looking surely at the political effect? Perhaps you can give me more detail than usual!

Ray: At first, there were fruitless discussions about who to exclude and sectarian rivalries emerged, but these soon gave way in practice to exciting co-operative ventures where it became obvious that we were all ploughing the same furrow. But what was the motivating force behind my initiatives? Memoirs are written with the benefit of hindsight and, all too often, a 'spin' is put on what was thought to have been said and acted upon. The brutal truth is probably only in the history recorded at the time, so the best answer might be in this extract from a speech I made to local government employees at a conference in Japan in October 1992, when I was invited to the International Conference of Nuclear-Free Zone Authorities. There was a workshop to discuss practial ways of campaigning for peace and I was asked to speak about what I was doing in Edinburgh that I had put down as my special concern or activity. After a general introduction I said:

"All cities have two faces - a shiny top and a shadowy bottom, and Edinburgh is no exception. The other side of our city of half a million shows a widening gap between the rich and the poor, increasing drugs and Aids problems, rising crime and unemployment, and chronic congestion from more and more private cars.The professional classes are also ill at ease with the situation. Many of them now vote Labour so that, for the first time in Edinburgh's history, the Labour Party gained control of the city's administration in 1984. Very often, a change in the political complexion of a council results in little change for the average citizen, as there is a lot of inertia to overcome. In any case, the British Government in London, through its Scottish secretary of state, has increased its control, especially financially, in the council's affairs. The new Labour Council of Edinburgh decided to publicise its efforts with a slogan, 'Improving Services, Creating Jobs'. They distributed broadsheets of information, opened up the City Chambers to local organisations, encouraged the setting up of community councils, and formed advisory committees with representatives of local organisations.

These measures have helped to remove some of the alienation of the population from the decision-making process. Access and accountability with freedom of information is sadly lacking in our so-called democracy, so I rated these changes as being significant, even though they did not make headline news. The present representative type of democracy is inadequate because it tends to encourage a paternalistic attitude by councillors, as they can make decisions with little need to consult. Pressures from existing vested interests often leads to an acceptance of the 'Establishment' view. Thus, the *status quo* is preserved. When change is needed in favour of those without the influence and power of property and money, a more radical type of democracy is required. Let me give you an example by showing how we have linked the peace movement with the council. Conservative and other politicians declare that issues of peace and security are the prerogative of central government and outside the remit of the local. However, during the Cold War, local authorities were obliged to organise systems of civil defence, build deep bomb-proof bunkers for officials and distribute information to all citizens in case of nuclear war with the USSR. Every householder was asked to store tins of beans and water under the stairs!. People were shown how to whitewash their windows to prevent incoming radiation and to stay in their houses until told by radio to do otherwise You, who are well aware of the consequences of even small, unsophisticated atomic bombs, may well laugh at such ridiculous instructions, but they were meant to get the population used to the idea that nuclear war was not only inevitable, but winnable.The peace organisations, together with the trades unions and labour movement, challenged the authorities on the details of such a policy. The Edinburgh Council proclaimed its intention to become a nuclear-free zone and turned its Emergency Planning Committee into an Advisory Committee on Peace Matters as a sub-committee of the Council. Thus, the policy of civil defence was exposed as a dishonest campaign, imposed on the local authority against its will. For forty years my main interest has been the Campaign for Nuclear Disarmament. Even though the

Cold War and the nonsense of civil defence are things of the past, today Britain's first of four giant Trident submarines is coming to Scotland, to be armed with a new generation of nuclear weapons, multiplying our nuclear capacity eightfold, at a time when the USA and Russia are decreasing theirs. Our reason is, of course, nothing to do with defence. It has never been the case. It stems from our imperial past and our rulers' 'Great Power' chauvinism, maintaining our permanent seat in the UN Security Council and other international bodies.So the essential element is the linkage of national to local concerns, and to involve more people and their organisations in the decision-making process.

I thus represented CND on the Advisory Committee and initiated the Edinburgh Peace Festival. An independent committee of organisations was formed, receiving financial assistance from the council. So what are its aims? Firstly, it aims to bring together those who want to build a civil society based on social justice, the peaceful settlement of disputes, religious and ethnic understanding, ecological responsibility and nuclear disarmament. Secondly, it provides events ranging from concerts to conferences, from displays to discussions, from exhibitions to entertainment, with national and international performers and speakers. Thirdly, it promotes the theme 'Think Globally, Act Locally', involving all sections of the community, linking individuals, grassroots organisations and decision-making bodies, advancing and not detracting from the identity of each.

I then explained to my audience that a mere representative type of democracy can lead to an elected dictatorship, the need for a more participatory type, and the adoption of a more pragmatic approach when the complexities of human behaviour are appreciated but not made the excuse for delaying action for the empowerment of individuals and their organisations. I concluded, then, by saying that: 'The end result is that by empowering more people, the whole of society benefits. Ordinary citizens will see the need to solve all problems by peaceful negotiation and are made familiar with the machinery necessary to achieve this. It has always seemed important to me that democratic centralism should not only be 'top down' but also 'bottom up' from grass roots level.'

Eric: I believe this was reported and together with the peace festivals it was welcomed you were highly commended by the City Council.

Ray: One of the proudest moment of my life was the presentation by the City of Edinburgh of the Sir William Y. Darling Award for Good Citizen of the Year 1988 in recognition of my work in the peace movement. I claimed at the time that this award reflected more honour on the Council than on me, for its recognition of the value of a strong peace movement in Edinburgh with which I was proud to be associated. I gave the money to the Peace Festival and I recall that Sir William Y. Darling had been a well-known Tory holding high office in a former administration not noted for his sympathies with any of the organisations with which I was associated. His nephew now the Rt. Hon Alistair Darling MP, former Chancellor of the Exchequer of the UK Government, told me, with his tongue in cheek, that his uncle would be turning in his grave if he had known that I had been a recipient of such an award! Thank you, Eric, for letting me tell the whole story.

Eric: Not at all. I was fascinated by it as I know a good number of CND members. What other activity at the time would you label as 'fruitful'?

Ray: I remember trying to fill in what I thought were gaps in the thinking of leading contributors to an international meeting on peace and security held over several days in Berlin in the GDR in June 1988. This is how I made my contribution as the delegate from the Scottish Committee of the Communist Party. After making some general comments. I said: I'd like to focus your attention on a different approach to 'development'. The key point is this. Human activity is now a major ecological factor - not yet fully appreciated, but well understood. The scale, acceleration and direction of growth of energy use and development are going to threaten rather than help the well-being of humanity as we move into the next century. Therefore, development must be shown to be sustainable. After several thousand generations of *Homo sapiens*, in my one lifetime world population has tripled. More importantly, urbanisation, industrialisation, soil erosion, pollution, depletion of non-renewable resources and the number of people living in poverty have increased manyfold. I then developed the theme of development and the seductive power of consumerism, attacking the 'more of everything' sloganeering of some of the participants. The UN Bruntland Report, 'Our Common Future', had just been published, and in conversation it was obviously not in the hands of the very people who were in a position to make decisions, including a minister from one of the African nations. Of course, in subsequent years, ever-increasing publicity and concern led to limited action by governments, but the Eastern bloc was as guilty as any in their views on sustainable development, and even now the concept is largely misunderstood. I designed an exhibition and a questionnaire on the environment and the Bruntland report and made a survey of opinion assisted by Lynne Devine, presenting a report to the Peace Forum which was then published. Since then, of course, the problems have been widely discussed in the media and 'green' movements have expanded.

Eric: Let's go back to the Gorbachov era in the USSR. Have you any comment on the changes then at the time of Peristroika and great changes in the CPSU?

Ray: You keep asking me to go back but I have been privileged with a number of informal meetings with comrades from the Soviet Union and especially with a delegation in 1987. I remember discussions with the Moscow police inspectors and asking how the police on duty are prevented from abusing their powers. In particular, we had an excellent exchange of views with members of the Central Committee of the Kiev Communist Party on the tendency for any bureaucracy to look first to its own interests before those they purported to serve, of the need to institutionalise checks and balances on those holding political power and for access to information which governments otherwise wrongly withhold in the name of 'national security' in order to avoid valid criticism. As an aside, I must say that I am often astonished that writers are supposedly able to quote verbatim from conversations held years previously - how he said one thing, and she replied another, ad infinitum! I suspect that it is all invented for effect because readers generally like a conversational style. I haven't followed this tradition until this example, which wasn't recorded, but was along the lines of what is set out below. Announcing that I came from Scotland where there was much discussion of the problems of nationalism and democracy, the conversation continued roughly as follows:

RAY: Why do Jews in the USSR have to state that fact on their passports?

1ST SEC: In the USSR there are many nationalities and this is stated on their passports.

RAY: Is not Judaism a religion and not a nationality?

1ST SEC: The Jews don't see it that way, especially the Zionists whose allegiance is first to the Jewish state of Israel and only second to the USSR.

RAY: Is your allegiance first to the Ukraine and secondly to the USSR?

1ST SEC: Probably increasingly so. (Smiles all round)

RAY: So are the many Russians in the Ukraine second class citizens?

1ST SEC: Of course not. They are our valuable partners.

RAY: But I detect a difference in attitude to Russians and Jews, but let me ask a further question. Is there not a problem with Moscow as the capital of Russia and also of the USSR?

1ST SEC: Why should there be? I don't understand.

RAY: Because it seems to many of us in Scotland that because London is the capital of England and also the capital of the United Kingdom they confuse Britishness, Englishness and Scottishness, and have inherited unconsciously the imperialist notion of imposing on us policies against our will. All federal states have found serious problems when the capital of the country wasn't the countried biggest city and deliberately much smaller such as Washington, Ottawa and Canberra, Brazilia, Abuja etc. Many people, I suspect, in your republics, see Moscow as Russian capital imposing a Russian will. Now supposing Leningrad had been made the capital of the union, separate from Moscow as capital of Russia...

CHAIRMAN: We don't see it that way as the republics are autonomous. Next question please.

Other members of the delegation asked questions on the role of women, the advantages of having a self-employed sector, problems of food production and distribution, and the separation of the Party from the State machine. Feedback from the interpreter the next day revealed that when we had gone there was a heated discussion on our comments; he mentioned that it was the first time after many years of interpreting that he had heard so many challenging remarks. I mention this because they gave as the excuse for a closed society the understandable security problem - their defence against the West was secrecy as well as arms. On the other hand, it enables those in power not to be challenged by the very real problems as they emerge, so that a kind of stagnation results and society loses out. Being on the sidelines meant that I was without influence, but I also know that the CPGB only slowly learnt of the excesses of oppression in the Soviet Union and China as they were revealed much later from authoritative sources rather than from 'enemy propaganda'. Nevertheless, the international department of the Party made its views known in private conversations and, in general, were welcome for what diplomats call 'frank and full discussions'. At the end of the day, however, the tail can't wag the dog.

Eric: That was again are very interesting insight for me as a Jew but can we move on?

Ray: One question remains. After the collapse of the Soviet Union and many of the communist parties, was my participation a wasted effort? I think not. The archives will show that the activities of the British Communist Party were overwhelmingly concerned with national and local problems that other British parties did not seem to be tackling with sufficient knowledge, understanding, commitment and vigour. The Communist Party of Great Britain, in contrast to the CPSU, was no place for anyone wanting a career in politics. Those people, and I have known many, went to the Labour Party and I don't blame them. Indeed I respect their attempts to get to where power lies, but some were merely opportunists and integrity often went out of the window. I could name names but that would not get us anywhere. I have benefited personally from the company of comrades whose devotion to the various struggles was exemplary and it showed in their attitudes to their fellow human beings. In other words it rubbed off and gave one a unique sense of purpose and a positive attitude to life in general. But inevitably the Communist Party was internationalist in outlook - we are our brother's keeper as there is only one human kind. We have the common problem of the rich in all countries getting together to devise policies that exploit the poor. In 1965 I was terribly saddened with the reports in the Morning Star, and ignored by the rest of the media, that over a million communists and trades union activists had been slaughtered in a terrible bloodbath when General Suharto overthrew the Suharto Government with the aid of Britain and the U.S.A. which led to thirty years of oppressive dictatorship, the details of which have now been revealed in *Web Of Deceit* by Mark Curtis. International solidarity was therefore required of us, and the Soviet Union had the only game in town, so we put solidairity first. The questions and doubts many had were a luxury, or so it seemed at the time, when the threat of nuclear annihilation was very real. For example, I found no difficulty in accepting both the unilateral approach of CND and the multilateral policy of the CPGB. For me, the priority was the same - to influence public opinion and galvanise people into action to stop the Government from fanning the flames of the nuclear arms race and to redeploy those resources for social use.

Eric: Let's be honest. There's no evidence for that except hearsay.

Ray: Now the archives in Moscow are revealing how near to collapse the Soviet system has been since its inception in 1917 and books are now being written from both sides of the equation – emphasising either the role of the key players like Lenin and Stalin or the circumstances which did not allow any other policies to be implemented.It seems to me that history confirms Marx's prerequisites for socialism being built out of the most advanced capitalist countries and not the most backward as in Russia. Also the 'domino effect' of world revolution did not take place. Indeed, counter-revolution and the suppression of communist parties everywhere have been the name of the game ever since 1917. The wars of intervention, civil strife, famine and economic collapse forced Lenin and then Stalin into extreme measures, initially to enable the socialist revolution to survive by progressively banning all opposition, and then by 'liquidating' even communists who were said by someone to be a 'dissident', so that an oppressive one-party state was built up. Oscar Lange, one of the socialist planners, said on his death bed, 'I would have been a Bukharinite gradualist (executed by Stalin before the war), yet as I think back, I ask myself, again and again, was there an alternative to the indiscriminate, brutal, basically unplanned rush forward of the first Five-Year Plan? Would the Romanovs, 'our allies in World War I', have built such an advanced industrial and literate state out of the ruins of a backward and peasant-based economy? Instead we can be grateful for its existence during World War II. As Eric Hobsbawm eloquently and authoritatively wrote in his seminal work *The Age of Extremes*, 'Only the temporary and bizarre alliance of liberal capitalism and communism in self-defence against world fascism saved democracy, for the victory over Hitler's Germany was essentially won, and could only have been won, by the Red Army.' Then in the post-war years the United States raised the stakes so high in the arms race that the USSR bankrupted itself and capitalism took over. Like the Miners' Strike of '84, the Soviet Union, in my opinion, was not going to be allowed to succeed WHATEVER THE COST. This, however, can be a reason for resistance and not submission, in what was formerly a key issue, the class struggle.

When Boris Yeltsin in 1990 replaced Gorbachev and his Perestroika policies to reform the USSR, he invited hundreds of American and British financial experts, negotiating secretly through his daughter as the go-between from the U.S. Embassy in Moscow to himself resulting in a free-for-all scramble to privatise the massive amount of state property. As a consequence Russia has become the most unequal developed country in the world. 7% of the population have become obscenely rich (the Billionaire Oligarchs some of whom live in London tax-free). 80% of the Russians now live in extreme poverty and male expectation of life has dropped from 71 years to 53 since Yeltsin's capitalist reforms. Also, the standards of health, culture and education have continued to fall since Soviet times as a result of the West's advice resulting in an atmosphere of no hope for the future.

Every communist party in every country was different because the political situations were different. I therefore viewed countries, like an individual human being, as one of great complexity and full of game plans and contradictions. May I suggest that Tape 8 is the crucial one?

Eric: I see why you think as you do but it's also what you are motivated to think and do, so put on Tape 8 please because when we recorded it I thought this was the best and most significant!

TAPE EIGHT: THE UNCERTAIN FUTURE IS POLITICAL

Eric: When did you give up as organiser of the Edinburgh Peace Festivals and can you summarize in a few sentences what has engaged you in politics since then.

Ray: I retired as co-ordinator of the Edinburgh Peace Festival in October 1993, after a memorable social evening and presentation at the Assembly Rooms. However, I continued to assist with certain events, especially the civic forum in 1995, and the Campaign for Scottish Democracy. The election of a Labour Government on the 1st May 1997 reflected a sea change in the mood of the British people for a more caring and sharing society. I doubt whether there was, in fact, much of a shift in that direction as Labour is still not challenging the Thatcherite policies that preceded it. In Scotland, however, the Tories were left with only one MP, no MEP's and no control of any council. Scotland gained a Parliament with vitriolic publicity against it about the costs showing yet again that they know the price of everything but the value of nothing. We are now moving to an Independence referendum with the Labour Party going further to the right in support of the status quo.

Eric: Before we discuss the question of Independence let's move on to some conclusions of the last few decades and prospects for the future.

Ray: It is of interest to me that researchers have confirmed the common sense conclusions that we need support if we are to have the necessary resilience to face anything that life throws at us. This support is not financial. It includes good relationships with our parents, appropriate connections with communities of interest or place. More importantly, it involves an external value system that goes beyond the welfare of ourselves, providing a feeling of purpose and meaning to our lives. Traditionally, religion has supplied the latter to much of mankind but the straight humanitarian and humanist approach avoids the dogmatism that has made so many religions destructive, as well as comforting, to those inheriting them. Thus, the personal must be social in the first instance. When decisions have to be made it becomes a political issue.Last century saw the best, but also the worst of man's achievements, and I have had the remarkable privilege of living through most of it, observing some of it and participating in a little. We are now in the 21st. century and it is time to take stock. Let us recall the subtitle of this work: 'What it means to be Human from the Local to the Global.' I now think that the words 'left' and 'right' are inadequate to describe the pluralist nature of the conflicting interests in society but have been historically meaningful. At the age of eighty six I have retired from organisational responsibilities, but it occurred to me that the evolution of my thoughts, decisions and actions may be of interest to others, especially to those who would like to put me into the psychiatrist's chair! I therefore jotted down my memories as they emerged of those decades. It is not a question of ferreting out all the errors and omissions for an extended and revised edition, even though this would not be without significance, for what we forget may also be something we would rather not remember. Professional authors rewrite their texts ten times over, embroidering and embellishing them to make them more attractive to the reader. I know that this draft lacks anecdotes and humour. It lacks humility, style and an explanation of what I really mean as I jump from one aspect to another. It lacks... but why go on? It is for others to judge my life, but I hope, instead, that these comments may provoke my grandchildren, friends, political acquaintances and others to think more generally of their implications and, by understanding a little more of the past, understand a little more of how they should face the future.

Eric: Would you agree that we are about to face a historical shift in the challenges that the world faces as globalisation races ahead and our idea of progress is shattered?

Ray: In these pages I have challenged the notion of inevitable progress. We may make personal progress in our acquisition of goods, knowledge and wisdom, and these can be made available to others. For example, there is no going back on our ideas of justice, human rights, animal welfare, the role of women, democratic participation and a scientific rather than a superstitious way of thinking. I have witnessed remarkable changes in the attitude and behaviour of men and women towards each other, derived in the first instance from the increased education and economic independence of women and, secondly, from the collective action of women. These changes have led, in turn, to a 'new man' free to express his inner feelings without being called a 'wimp'. Also, my own thoughts about world affairs have changed but I can point to no one event and say, 'It was then that I changed my mind.' I hope that these chapters have shown that I have matured through time, experience and reflection and that you should now begin to know what made me tick. But the crucial question is, 'Has the collective wisdom and behaviour of humanity as a whole increased?' I doubt it. Like the holiday crowds that destroy the peace and beauty of places that attracted them in the first place, we are also destroying Planet Earth and jeopardising the well-being of future generations. There is little sign of the political will necessary to alleviate the abject poverty, misery, inequality, ill-health and ignorance into which the majority of mankind is born.

Eric: What has the twentieth century meant for you and how do you see the future?

Ray: For me, the entering the 21st. century has meant a lot. I see myself as one link in a chain of generations. I have, at last, found out what life is all about. Life is a struggle. It may be for the individual or for the species. It may be Darwinian or humanitarian. The issues are always more complex than we realise but people also say this when they want to avoid decision and action. I've had my crack of the whip and I am now content that I have lived my life to the full despite the contradictions, split loyalties and disappointments. I would hope that I haven't hurt anyone, but I know I must have done. I've grown up in my relationships, but not soon enough. Most important for me is that I did what I could at the time - and not just for myself. I am happy that I feel that I've had a life fulfilled. I enjoyed making a bold attempt at realising my potential in as many aspects of life as possible. Not being talented in any one aspect, I benefited from a wealth of influences and experiences, from art, music, drama and study, to teaching, travel, gardening and sailing. This is important inasmuch as the previous chapters may have given the impression that my life was spent getting in and out of politics and relationships! Indeed, the ordinariness of my daily routine has been as self-fulfilling as the more colourful days of organising successful events, meeting celebrities or leading the way in geographical fieldwork. If nothing else, I hope that these pages show that ordinary people can live extraordinarily interesting, exciting and purposeful lives. In my youth I was shy and socially ill at ease, but I was enthusiastic about 'finding out', and this put me in a position of having to change, sometimes superficially overriding my basic character traits. My grasp was always less than my reach however, as I did not always persist long and hard enough in any one direction. Hence, I regard myself as the same person, with the same nagging conscience, as seventy years ago, but with a much more open personality, less impetuous and more contented with my lifestyle.

Throughout my life the personal has been linked to the social and political, and my attitude reflected the twentieth century hope that the world could be made a better place by the application of rational thought, leading to the increasing harmony and welfare for all its billions of people, half of whom currently live in squalor and misery, while a small minority are obscenely rich, and getting richer on the wealth produced by the former. The globalisalion of the capitalist market has been accompanied by the collapse of the countervailing influence that the Soviet Union may have had, leading to the world domination of the International Monetary Fund and the dollar even though the USA is heavily in debt. Countries can now no longer control their own economies. There is an aggressive 'winner takes all' philosophy which is gaining strength. For example, in 1965 the ratio of the wealth of the top twenty per cent to the bottom twenty per cent was thirty to one. Now it is eighty to one.

Eric: The counter-claim is that there is a trickle-down effect and that even if the wealth of the rich were spread evenly it would be spread so thinly as to be insignificant.

Ray: This is not so. 'Facts are chiels that winna ding', as the Scots say. If the world's three hundred and fifty-eight multi-billionaires were to distribute their riches amongst the poorest part of the world's population, (some two billion, seven hundred million individuals) they would each double their income! It would not be much, but think of what it would mean for their survival, welfare and quality of life. Unfortunately, that's not going to happen. The world's capitalist economy is expanding and becoming more exploitative. An example of how it works was shown by Dave Phillips of the San Francisco Earth Island Institute, writing about the Californian tuna industry. (*New Internationalist*, February 1997). 'In the old days,' he said, 'California had the largest tuna-canning industry in the world, but today - these are approximate figures - the wages in California were about seventeen dollars an hour. So the industry moved, first to Puerto Rico, where wages were about seven dollars an hour, and then, when they decided that was too much, to American Samoa, where wages were about three dollars fifty an hour. From there it moved to Ecuador, where workers were paid about four dollars an hour, and then on to Thailand, where a great deal of the industry is today, and wages are four dollars a day! And now, amazingly enough, there is some movement to Indonesia, where wages are as low as two dollars a day.' Low, of course, because there is a dictatorship keeping protest down, with the help of arms exported by Britain, France and the United States. This is the real reason for 'aid'. The IMF makes it a condition of lending that the recipient countries reduce expenditure on education, health and welfare, but not on arms imports. Yet, only one per cent of the world's expenditure on arms would be sufficient to educate the eighty per cent of the world's children not at school. Another one per cent would enable everyone to have access to clean water that would remove the shame of allowing a child to die every three seconds from preventable diseases. Think of the cost of a useless Trident or the 90 billions of tax lost in tax havens.

Eric: So what, how and when should we now be demanding?

Ray: The present economic system cannot reform itself and there is no indication that a Labour government will have the political will to do any better so watch out for more of the same in 2015. I once thought that the ideas of socialism would be contagious and, through mass struggle, would eventually lead to them becoming an unstoppable force and so improve the quality of life of all. I was wrong. The disorder, instability, fragmentation and unpredictability of the human condition echoed the physicist's 'chaos theory' rather than Marx's rationale of progress. Marx was, however, correct in concluding that it is not the consciousness of men that determines their being but, on the contrary, their social being that determines their consciousness so the understanding persists.

Eric: What our blind friend wants to know are your conclusions after such a long life of left-wing activity.

Ray: To summarise what I now think, it seems to me that we are locked into a global capitalist economy with hierarchical, aggressive and competitive societies, which may or may not be producing more consumer goods, but are certainly increasing the 'feel-bad' factor. The information superhighway is accelerating the take-up of consumerism and irrationalism that, if continued, can only lead to catastrophe - just read the United Nation's report 'Our Common Future', and the many other publications on the rapidly changing face of our planet if you want to know whether or not this is sensationalism! Let's go back to 1997. What was the future that was being forecast by the Labour, Liberal and Conservative parties? It wasn't only the Green Party and the left that was critical. George Soros, the world's leading financier who makes and loses billions in any one week, says (*New Statesman 1997*) that one day the global financial market will collapse into chaos unless we find 'some international legally binding financial co-operation to match the globalisation of markets.' The danger, it seems to me, is that any future proposal to the UN will be too little and too late without a massive global movement to campaign for it. We are now at the beginning of the twenty first century when every previous decade has seen the doubling of previous knowledge, but unfortunately not of wisdom. The twentieth century saw world population multiplied fourfold, urban population sixfold, the consumption of energy and non-renewable resources tenfold - an acceleration of events affecting the world ecosystem and which our planet will be unable to sustain. It took a million years for the world's population to reach two billion in 1927, the year of my birth. It will have tripled in my own short lifetime! 9% of all the people who have ever lived through the thousands of years of settled existence are living NOW!

Eric: Can you give some examples of present trends that threaten the planet as our only place to live and whether we are fitted to do something about the problems?

Ray: Global warming will result in rising sea levels and more climatic extremes. The hole in the ozone layer will cause more skin cancers and wildlife extinctions. The world is losing more than seven million hectares of fertile land each year to soil degradation and erosion. Clean water is now more expensive than oil in many countries and will be a source of international conflict as supplies of both dry up. Car production and pollution, already approaching saturation levels, will double in the next two decades. The list grows longer, as does the lip service paid to it, while the movement of economic migrants is already threatening regional stability. John Cleese has said that prolonged chaos in society is worse than organised wickedness! We are no longer talking about a new utopia, but about *survival.* What the existing political structures cannot prioritise is that PEOPLE NEED PEOPLE. Instead, we are being seduced into thinking only of acquiring consumer goods to the exclusion of other values. Too many people are encouraged to think that they can join the few winners instead of the many losers.

Eric: Yet the people I meet know that there is something wrong, but feel impotent to do anything about it. We are also encouraged to recycle waste paper, cans and bottles and give generously to 'Third World' charities.

Ray: No one doubts their value, but it is only applying sticking plasters where major surgery is required. At present we are like rabbits caught in the headlights of a car, unable to move. As the *Scotsman* columnist, James Hunter, wrote in January 1997, 'When a plausible replacement for capitalism - in the shape of Marxist-inspired socialism and communism - seemed to be waiting just off-stage, it made good sense, even to capitalism's most fervent proponents, to minimise joblessness, poverty and the like. But now that there is no alternative waiting in the wings - no readily believable alternative, at any rate - to capitalism, this most productive, most inventive, but also most voracious and exploitative of economic systems, can safely be let rip in a fashion not seen since the early nineteenth century.' Therefore, slogans for world revolution will go unheeded, but we can, at least, defend the gains already made, promote a new vision for the younger generation, and appeal, in the first instance, to the enlightened and longer term self-interest of the richer minority. Let them know that if they resist a reform of the system they themselves will be caught up with the problems of disease, instability and violence breaking out as the pot boils over. Along with many of my generation, I thought that education, not merely schooling, would lead to a greater feeling of responsibility and therefore of political involvement by more and more people. This, in turn, would lead to the development of a mature civic society that would not allow a government to do otherwise than prioritise social need over private greed. Some pointed to Scandinavia as an example. Others, like myself, thought that social change had to go much further if the resistance offered by the established forces was to be overcome.

Eric: You are getting pessimistic again. What of the future for your grandchildren?

Ray: My conclusion is that if we are to make the 21st. century a real turning point in man's turbulent history, we have got to think laterally and imaginatively, but, at the same time, be realistic about the nature of the beast - man! I think it was Confucius who said that learning without thinking is useless but thinking without learning is dangerous. Can we involve more people and politicians to take the longer view and not just the next election? It has always seemed to me that theory and practice must go together, and that pragmatism must accompany principle. However, we have an abundance of untenable beliefs that, far from making paths, are blocking the way through to inspiring experiences that are capable of lifting individuals and groups to even greater heights by inhibiting the baser instinctive reactions. A real and worthwhile education must, in my opinion, develop a sense of connection with the rest of the universe in a pleasurable and harmonious way - an ecological approach which should affect the way we think about our place within a giant support system. Only then can we begin to understand how the intricate, complex and beautiful patterns of life work. We may not know why, but we can certainly try and know how, and this has been my fascination with a scientific rather than a superstitious view of the world and its peoples which has intrigued me all my life. I am left with more questions than answers, but a rational view is the only route through to man's survival and his enjoyment of it. That is why I have joined the Green Party and 'Yes' campaign for an independent Scotland and others!

Eric: It seems to me that it is not only so-called progressive people who have a logical mind. You cannot show that most people are now going to support the Green Party.

Ray: Of course, the conservative view can also be rationalised. 'Human nature won't change.' It's a question of the survival of the fittest and the devil takes the hindmost. As Thatcher succinctly put it, 'You can't buck the market' and 'There's no such thing as society'. All values are therefore based on competition and possessive individualism. 'The less fortunate should get off their backsides and elbow their way in if they can.' 'Their problem is not ours and is not on our agenda for discussion, let alone action.' You have heard these time and again! This kind of reasoning is very convenient for those who assume that their wealth, power and privileges have been ordained by God. Why, then, should they care about the world's poor and oppressed unless it hits their pocket? One reason is that it is in their long-term interest but they have not yet been forced to think beyond this year's balance sheet.

Eric: Ray, Give me a rational rather than a polemical explanation of what you are saying?

Ray: I summarised this at the meeting of the Scottish Progressive Philosophy Group in 1996. It is this: If animals don't do the right thing they don't survive, so they tune in very accurately and sensitively to the real world around them. Humans are very much more sophisticated and have the capacity to delude themselves as they struggle to match their emotional and intellectual responses.

Briefly, the lower parts of the brain are programmed from birth so that we can operate on automatic for much of the time. However, the higher parts involve a learning process, becoming actively engaged in making billions of interconnections in the construction of a very complex model of the world from the images it has received from a highly selected array of messages identified by the sense receptors. At about one hundred thousand years ago, there was a remarkable evolutionary jump with the development of symbolic language as opposed to the concrete associations of animal communication. The new abstract model of the world now inside our heads is the key to self-knowledge, knowing who we are, what we are and the how and why of our behavioural patterns.This model is then used for comparison when there is further input, leading to action or its internalisation that we call thinking and imagining, but this often comes into conflict with our baser instincts of fear, lust, jealousy, envy, passion, greed, aggression and so on. How often does our intellect accept something that our heart doesn't, and vice versa? How often do people confuse reality with the symbols which only represent parts of reality? How often do religious leaders use metaphors to mystify rather than clarify the moral issues of the day? How often do people confuse religion as a belief in the supernatural with the humanistic needs of ritual, morality, dignity and entertainment? The problem, as I see it, is how is it possible to increase the proportion of our lives propelled by rational, long-term and global considerations, rather than the irrational, short-term and individualised ones? One of the biggest hurdles to its solution is the Platonist-dualist approach that has bedevilled thinking throughout history, that of separating mind from matter, of the natural as against the supernatural; that is, treated as if they were quite separate entities, and not only separate, but with the assumption that there is an authority or deity with a mind of its own outside ourselves which becomes a useful tool to rule us. This figment of our fertile imagination is conveniently reinforced by élites and their reactionary ideologies. On the other hand, the Aristotelian pragmatic view that mind cannot work except within, and as a function of, a living brain, leads to a more democratic, scientific and healthy society.

Eric: Isn't that an oversimplication? Religions have always been with us?

Ray: I know it is an oversimplification to say it, but it seems to me that religion, superstition, legend, cults and mystical philosophies have been instrumental in retarding human progress, but have been part of the human condition because they answer a human need. However, a belief in the supernatural thrives on ignorance and a lack of understanding about what motivates people, and the divisiveness of religions is used by the power-brokers of society in their attempt to perpetuate the *status quo* and its privileged élite. It can be argued that even the most intelligent can be drawn into a belief of the supernatural. Why? I think it is because we are the only species gifted with the knowledge of our eventual demise - and we don't like it so like a drowning man we try and grasp at any straw! We therefore hope and wishfully think that there must be more to it than that, and invent a life after death rather than admit what we now know of all living things - they all decompose and are recycled with only memories left in others. I say this in a dialectical sense and not in a reductionist or mechanical mode. We are ignorant of what makes self-consciousness and many other aspects, but study, rather than magical conclusions, is the only way to resolve the problems and discover the truth of the matter. In marked contrast to the mumbo-jumbo uttered at many religious funerals, the following quote by Boris Pasternak is often given at humanist ones and points the way to a much greater understanding of what we are: 'However far back you go in your memory, it is always in some external active manifestation of yourself that you come across your identity - in the work of your hands, in your family, in other people... this is what you are. This is what your consciousness has breathed and lived on and enjoyed throughout your life. your immortality, your life in others. And what now? What does it matter to you if, later on, it is called your memory? This will be you - the real you - that enters the future and becomes part of it.'

Eric: I like that quote. I must note it down and pass it on! Continue your speech!

Ray: 'Humans are tremendously creative and imaginative, producing, not only religious dogma, but also great works of art, music, drama, literature, poetry and, lest we forget, some elegant and beautiful hypotheses in science. Let us capitalise on this. We are rational inasmuch as we can reason, but at the same time we are all driven by instinctive desires and wishes, programmed to survive as an individual and as a species. Many are unaware of these powerful drives, and, as Freud and others have shown, we bury the real reasons for our actions and substitute others. The responses may be plausible to the individual, but they are also flawed and objectively irrational, producing problems rather than solving them' I then presented to the group, examples of the political implications of this view of mankind and the dangers inherent in the apparent need for 'authority' - a god, a good czar, a leader, a father figure, and media-made icons. I ended by saying: 'The question is - to what extent is our future going to be decided by reasoned dialogue, consensus and agreement or by emotive and instinctive reactions with arguments derived from private and exclusive belief systems? I suggest that *we have to cope with an interplay of both.*'

Eric: Now let us think of a different problem. Can we discuss our hopes for our grandchildren who may be influenced now by the media rather than our opinions?

Ray: News, whether good or bad, is now part of the entertainment industry but who controls what we see and hear? In 1991, 50 huge companies dominated the world's output. Now, 20 years later, there are seven. They are AOL Time-Warner, the Disney Corporation, Bertlesmann, Viacom, Murdoch's News Corporation, as well as Sony and Vivendi. Together these companies are worth over 200 billion just because you want it and they have swallowed up the rest even though their former names may have been kept. These megacorporations exist to make a profit from human aspirations and weaknesses and to perpetuate the very status quo that has made them wealthy. The result is that hundreds of different cultures are now being repackaged throughout the world mainly in terms of the American values, styles of consumerism and entertainment. I don't think you need me to spell out the results of this promotion of instant gratification - the attitude to life of "I want it and I must have it now". People are persuaded that enough is **not** enough. Much wants more. This style of life is affecting everybody and everywhere. Are there not serious consequences for our **quality** of life especially as we squander the limited non-renewable resources by companies that know the cost of everything but the value of nothing?

Eric: That's entertainment as they say but what about useful products like food?

Ray: Think of the land we are bequeathing our children. For example, we have had the industrialisation of world agriculture with the aid of millions of tons of fertilisers, herbicides, pesticides and hormonal and chemical additives to animal feed together with GM and new seed varieties. Output has therefore kept pace with world population up to the present but is unlikely to do so in the future. Also, its products have been cornered by the rich nations leaving only crumbs for the poor. You would have noticed in the supermarkets that most of the vegetables, fruit and flowers have been imported such as potatoes from Egypt, green beans from Kenya and carnations from Bolivia. They are growing them to pay the interest on their debts but with the consequence of rapidly decreasing the area of good land available for their own subsistence crops and rising prices in the village markets. There is an illusion in the West that development aid means that there is a net flow of capital into the poor countries whereas the opposite is the case with over $200 million net going to the rich G8 countries every day! Are we not causing problems rather than solving them?

Eric: Who do you think influences our cultural and economic situation other than ourselves as free individuals? Big Corporations? The Government?

Ray: The lead is being taken by the United States with less than 5% of the world's population consuming 25% of the world's resources and President Bush stated that he will never agree to any curb on the United States' economic development, growth and the importation of the cheapest raw materials and oil. This overides every other consideration. But his so-called "national interest" is not, of course, for the 42 million Americans without medical insurance, nor for the 30 million in a recent study published by Tufts University of Massachusetts who " live in households that are experiencing hunger and food insecurity" while the obscenely rich get even richer. Is it not even in the long-term interest of the USA itself to change its policies? When George Bush announced that he was engaged "in a fight to save the civilised world", he was assuming powers and responsibilities of the United Nations which he does not possess. If we look at the total picture we can conclude that it is mainly the policies of the United States that are putting the world further into the mire instead of helping to get us out of it.

Eric: So you put all the blame on America?

Ray: Of course not, but it is the major culprit, forcing others to acquiesce. A growing number of Americans who know this but are not yet sufficiently confident to campaign. However, there is an increasing awareness that globalisation, international competition and organisations like the World Trade Organisation have reduced the power of national governments to the status of servile supporters of a voracious capitalist system which may be producing more consumer goods but also more inequality, stress, waste and a feel-bad factor of frustration and cynicism. Money now supersedes morality as the aim in life. Runaway capitalism feeds on six of the seven deadly sins of selfishness, greed, pride, envy, covetousness, and lust for power, perhaps leaving the seventh, sloth, to the aristocracy living on inherited wealth. This ideology affects us all and Michael Kelly in the Scotsman described how the electorate has become more "narrow, selfish and brutally short-sighted". Young people are opting out of party politics and the media blames individuals and never the economic and political system.

Eric: Aren't you omitting the vast opportunities opened up by the internet for ordinary people to share their ideas and enabling them to bypass the political parties as we have seen in the big anti-capitalist demonstrations that have taken place worldwide?

Ray: The information superhighway and the remarkable expansion and availability of knowledge with instant communication could lead to a flowering of democratic expression and action around the world and the global actions you mention are significant. However, it seems to me that the commercial world dominates the scene and retards progress in this direction, thus limiting its great educational and democratic potential. It is also true that much progress has been made in the general attitudes to minorities, children, the disabled and especially to women's issues and their status and role in society, mainly through mass campaigning over the years. Many studies have shown that the reduction of family size and the improvement in health and quality of life in poorer countries such as Cuba and the Indian State of Kerala have been due to government implementation of socialist policies giving priority to the education of women. Also, increasing numbers of people are releasing themselves from traditional dogmas and religious bigotry but the gap is often filled with less desirable irrational beliefs as an easier option to struggling to increase their self-knowledge with more permanent intellectual, imaginative and spiritual needs.

Eric: So you agree with me that we are, in fact, making some progress on balance?

Ray: Not, on balance, in the 21st. century world we are talking about. Yes, we live longer. Infectious diseases once the scourge of civilisations have been seriously tackled in the West but now diseases of affluence take their toll. In the "South" the most important investment that could be made in terms of cost-benefit is the piping of clean water but development too often means investment in the profit-making capital projects involving the multinationals and local corrupt practices. We are relieved by the absence of the threat of war on our own doorstep but it is worth reminding ourselves that Britain maintains its position at the top of the European league in arms expenditure as a percentage of GNP but is near the bottom of the league in health expenditure, a fact that is never put to the politicians interviewed on television. We should also remind ourselves of the proxy wars that have killed more people since World War Two than during it and the United Nations Organisation has been kept too weak by great power chauvinism to tackle the causes of war. It is now over 20 years since the end of the Cold War and the United States still has sixty one major bases in nineteen countries worldwide complete with hundreds of thousands of troops, planes and advanced weapons, including nuclear. More widespread throughout the world are the US Joint Combined Exchange Training Schemes and CIA infiltration, as for example, in all South and Central American countries except Cuba where they are confined to the illegally occupied Guantanamo Bay Area. It is not a coincidence that the scale of military penetration corresponds to that of the U.S. multinational corporations. We are therefore not solving social problems by military action but by denying these material and intellectual resources for civilian use we are exacerbating them. But all of us are involved here. Why do we allow a trillion dollars a year to be spent globally by the arms industries when this leads to weapons getting into the wrong hands but the further impoverishment of the two billion already living in misery. Is this progress or regression?

Eric: So there are major problems of poverty, social justice, war and certainly of democratic participation but we can surely take the necessary remedial action as these issues are taken up by NGOs and the politicians who want to popularise them?

Ray: Our rapid technological advances have led us to believe that there is a technical fix for any of our problems. This approach is now coming unstuck. Of all the problems we face, I think that the ecological threat is the worst because there are inherent difficulties and contradictions. Changes in climatic regimes, sea levels and vegetation zones have always taken place over long periods of time but never at the present accelerating pace, making it impossible for the biosphere to adapt quickly enough. To ameliorate the problem requires long-term planning and a redeployment of resources at variance with people's perceived interests and the over-riding concern of business with this year's balance sheet as the target. Of course, individuals as well as large corporations think occasionally of the long term but only if this coincides with their immediate aims. Hopefully, young people are more and more aware of the ecological threats but the response by governments is still in terms of sticking plasters rather than major surgery. The couple calling at the recycling bins on the way to buying a bigger car are congratulated for doing their bit to save the world! Also people are more likely to blame the social conflicts arising out of environmental degradation on causes other than man-induced climate change. This mirrors race, religion and migration being given as the reasons for social unrest rather than the underlying economic and class inequalities. For instance, the call for more "growth" is almost universal. I therefore responded to a feature article in the Scotsman as follows: "George Kerevan may be right in his assertion that global wealth has increased by one third in the last decade but I'm afraid most of this has gone to the already obscenely rich while the number living in misery has increased to over two billion. More importantly for all of us, he sees this accelerating growth as a god worth worshipping whereas it is leading us to climate change and ecological disaster."

Eric: So is it mainly a matter of educating our betters?

Ray: We are not only faced with ignorance, escapism and cynicism but also with a cultural mindset of denial. For example, in a book by Jeremy Leggart, a recognised authority on the oil industry, he relates why he defected to Greenpeace as their scientific advisor. He was once at dinner with BP's chief geologist, David Jenkins, who was puzzled by his concern over the rise of CO2 in the atmosphere whereupon Leggart produced the facts and figures. Jenkins showed his great surprise yet he was one of the people influencing policy. Let me quote Leggart. "The most basic information on the global-warming debate was not getting through to people like Jenkins. I had a similar experience at the World Climate Conference where I had been involved in a public debate with BP's managing director. It seemed that a kind of subtle corporate information shield was at work. People in the carbon-fuel industries were able to exchange perceived wisdoms about global warming... without the insertion of worrying extraneous information." Most of us who have expressed opposition to nuclear weapons to those involved, or about poverty to those living in luxury, recognise the willingness of people wielding power to turn a blind eye to such evils and it appears that they convince themselves. It almost seems endemic within those self-selected groups. They seem to exist in a comfortable and mutually supporting milieu not knowing how other people think and live. On the other hand, if the evidence and pressure gets to them, some are neutralised in their loyalty to their in-group and a few become allies in the cause of wider sections of society.

Eric: Does it have to be that way?

Ray: No. We are essentially **moral** animals. Available to us are language, abstract thought, knowledge, wisdom and a conviction that we can change the situation given the political will, a hard struggle and the organisations prepared to aim for Mount Everest and not merely Ben Nevis as we intervene to check the power of the established elites and achieve a more equitable regime with a different set of values. Cynicism and disillusionment derive from ignorance and a feeling of impotence. Therefore any movement that counters this should be encouraged. My own thinking has been informed, but not dictated by, that of Marx, Darwin, Freud, Gramci and contemporary thinkers like Kenan Malik and Steven Rose. My starting point was the statement by Marx that philosophers have only interpreted the world in different ways whereas the real task is to change it. In studying what can and cannot be changed I think we must also refer to people like Darwin and Freud. The three of them revealed that we are ineluctably involved in conflict and struggle in common with all living things but we are unique in that we can look objectively at the world outside ourselves and change it for the benefit of our fellow human beings. But now we must look to what young people are saying. While political systems may modify our suffering and improve the human condition to a limited extent, political parties alone can never significantly change the present trends quickly enough. Thinking is hard work and sometimes disappointing as the truth is not always what we want it to be. Self-deception is often comforting. It may also result in a certain fatalism and less, rather than more, commitment whereas at a minimum level we can always light a candle instead of cursing the darkness.

Eric: Nicely put but sounds rather difficult for busy people. Also, Is that all we can do?

Ray: No, but the longest road starts with one first step in the right direction. More than that, we can devise new sub-systems in society that can promote the best and ameliorate the worst. It is then necessary to persuade others that it is in the interest of everybody in the long term to live in a world with more social justice. But you can't make an omelets without breaking eggs so we come back to the earlier statement that we cannot be all things to all men. Take nothing at its face value. **QUESTION THE MOTIVES and not merely the words** of those who have achieved wealth, power and privilege under the present system. They say the things that they think you want to hear but it is essential to see through the rhetoric. They are going to fight hard to perpetuate the status quo. Social justice demands that the vested interests of the rich and powerful must be challenged by political pressure on a world scale and by democratic struggle at a community level. Evidence suggests that the negative effects of globalisation can be countered by building alliances in action and an emphasis on local involvement. There are an amazingly large number of local voluntary organisations and community groups with democratic structures beavering away on a range of single issues. Civil society is alive and kicking against an over-centralised system. Nowadays we can use the

Web and lobbying through websites like Avaaz. You reminded me last time that the only direct democracy was that of Athens - and it excluded women, slaves and foreigners! What we have today is the right of the citizen to be misinformed and to determine policy as long as it is what he is told. Hence my plea to "Think globally, act locally" and to organise the struggle accordingly.

Eric: These are surely generalisations that are meaningless for many people and you seem to flit easily from one debating point to another. Can you explain what you mean?

Ray: Joyce McMillan put it succinctly in her article in the Scotsman. "....new political movements in Britain and across the globe are raising questions that cannot be ignored - questions which, in fact, bear only a distant relation to the old socialist discourse of the 19th. and 20th. centuries.

They are questions about environment, intimacy, community, creativity, love, laughter, good food, and the quality of life under 21st century conditions; and the grey-faced managerialists of our corporate culture - and their pale imitators in the public service - have no idea how to deal with them. But insofar as we look to government for the big picture of where our society is going and why, these will increasingly be the questions that successful 21st century politicians will have to address. They will have, in other words, to give us less of that tired business-suit stuff about prudence and ambition; and more about how, after the age of cold-eyed materialism through which we have passed, we can get on with the business of building a 21st century society worth the name, a society based on trust, conviviality, and a rigorous sense of human values..." But how do we "get on with the business of building..." if we ignore the way that the present economic system undermines every effort of people to seek these higher human values?

Eric: But according to you the question remains; "**How** do you think that we can change the global capitalist system if it is the main obstacle to the building of a more just society?"

Ray: Perhaps the word "capitalism", like "socialism", is too general to be useful. Market forces should be used to produce toys, shoes and biscuits but not for health, education and water supplies. International agreements are needed to control the movement of capital and the operation of the multinationals but I agree that I haven't offered a blueprint for the society we should be aiming for. In my humble opinion we also need a second "Enlightenment" because the future can no longer be a mere continuation of the past. I think it is irresponsible not to accept the challenge, to analyse the facts and to plan ahead but human beings tend to let the long term look after itself until there's a catastrophe on a grand scale such as a world war or an ecological disaster. **A catastrophe may be the necessary catalyst for change** but if we are not prepared, evil forces can make the running. If we *are* prepared, our inherent humanity bubbles up, the big issues are tackled, resources are suddenly found and revolutionary ideas emerge and are acted upon. We have strong social instincts and we tend to feel and take action on behalf of our less fortunate brothers when they are in trouble. But why wait for the catastrophe with its accompanying human misery instead of responding now to the wake-up call? Movements and struggles go on and those who participate are rewarded by an authentic life worth living. It may well be that these spurious thoughts put down on paper by a no more than an ordinary mortal could be replicated by a million others.

Eric: I now see your letters regularly in the press about the campaign for a 'Yes' vote in the Independence Referendum in September 2014. The papers are full of scaremongering stories but very briefly, what is the basic claim of the YES campaign?

Ray: I can do no better than quote their initial statement. "Today, we have a government in Westminster that most of us did not vote for, and yet that government is able to make major decisions that impact on families and communities in Scotland against their wishes. As an independent country we will always get the government Scotland chooses – for instance, a government to use our £8 billion share of defence spending more wisely as Scotland is not seen as wanting to police the rest of the world.

The choice will be ours. We will be able to make Scotland the country we all know fairer and richer and it can benefit from its different history and social aspirations... In other words, Scotland must continue its own more positive path different from that of England. We have the resources in Scotland, offshore oil and green power, to take forward policies designed to meet the needs of all the people in Scotland and not just a minority.

We can elect the government we think cares most about Scotland – a government that will look after the interests of people living here in an interdependent world. For example, we could choose to reverse the UK government's tax cut for the very wealthiest in society and instead use the revenue from our vast offshore renewable energy that will come to Scotland, allowing us to benefit communities across the country.

We can work more effectively to attract companies to Scotland, and help businesses already here grow, allowing us to create more jobs. And, while the UK government plans to spend £100 billion on new nuclear weapons in the years ahead, we can choose to use our £8 billion share of this money more wisely.

The choice will be ours. We will be able to make Scotland the country we all know it can be, given the vote to start the negotiations. Scotland, known and admired all over the world could use its influence other countries as an honest broker in international disputes…

Eric: I like your optimism but this is my last question. Do you really think that sufficient people will campaign for an authentic life worth living and all that that contains? You have already addressed the contrariness and contradictions inherent in the human condition.

Ray: Yes, you have a got a point there. Some years ago, when Adlai Stevenson was a presidential candidate in America, someone in the audience declared, 'Every thinking man and woman in the United States is behind you', to which Adlai replied, 'But I don't want those. I want a majority', and, of course, he didn't get it. The media saw to that! Democracy and a life worth living are delicate plants and its price is eternal vigilance and struggle to remove ignorance.In particular, I am NOT saying that until everybody agrees with me nothing can be done - just the opposite! We have got to recognise people for what they are and society for what it is. I have always believed that what we have in common is greater than what divides us, so let a hundred different flowers bloom. We are all enriched by the pluralist nature of our communities, but let us not bow to those interested in destroying them. It is for this reason that I have found no difficulty in helping to develop campaigns and projects with men and women of goodwill from all walks of life, especially those of a religious persuasion. Many different people have inspired my life, but so too have I been inspired by the story of evolution, the beauty of the landscape, the wonders of the night sky and the challenge of the sea.

So perhaps we might despair unnecessarily as we seek a better life for all and I am reminded again of Gramsci's edict that the pessimism of the intellect can be overcome by the optimism of the will. The younger generation always had that optimism. The will to change things for the better is always there. Everybody has a set of ideas inside them and as the Chinese say, "The palest ink is more influential than the greatest memory." It is too important to leave to the professionals... Continue the dialogue, Start writing! start campaigning! Can this lead us to a better tomorrow? I hope so.

END

APPENDIX

OTHER MISCELLANEOUS TALKS AND LETTERS

I have selected a wide range of different topics that I have presented on different occasions over recent years but read them in any order you wish!

On Humanism

Eric: You say that you have lived a non-religious life yet from what I know you have always engaged in struggle against "man's inhumanity to man" and his endeavour to seek the best aspects of education, attitudes and morality. How would you describe 'non-religious' in a more positive way than atheism?

Ray: I would say I'm a humanist, recognising that there is something special and significant about homo sapiens that is inherently fascinating as a highly developed social animal and religion is found in all societies even though they look very different. Yes, we are part of the animal "kingdom" but distinguished from the other species by our ability to use abstract thought through symbolic language. Thus we are able to construct a whole variety of alternative worlds in our own imagination in terms of past, present and future, and hold a dialogue with those around us of amazing complexity. But as we remove the veils of ignorance an increasing number find that they do not need to invent a supernatural world and gods and goddesses to explain it. Yes, our search for the truth is often frustrating but there is no need to take the easy way out invoking "mystery" as a conversation stopper. Thinking instead there being only one natural universe to explore is liberating, worthwhile, purposeful and inspiring; giving, a rich tapestry of meaning to our lives provoking many other delightful questions to plague us!

Eric: But it seems me that people don't analyse religion as you have done. They just feel it and want it. It is not the intellectual exercise that you describe.

Ray: I agree. Our mental life, now that we have the luxury of time to reflect, is not just an intellectual exercise. It should be construed more broadly with the potential of all human beings in terms of our conscious experiences, emotions, sensations, thoughts, beliefs, feelings, hopes and aspirations, fears, desires, choices and decisions. This mental life is organically part of, and never separated from the rest of an individual, as throughout the rest of nature from the "lowest" to the "highest" form of life.

We must remind ourselves that evolutionary changes have taken place over such an enormous amount of time that talking about a billion years of geological time cannot be properly appreciated by the human mind that barely understands one lifetime! However, we now know and understand enough to realize how it works through natural selection with qualitative jumps, to reject entirely the "creationism" invoked by past ignorance.

On Emotional Intelligence

Aristotle said that anyone can become angry - that is easy but to be angry with the right person, to the right degree, at the right time, for the right purpose and in the right way - this is not easy. Rational people like academics often do irrational things because intelligence as it is presently defined has nothing to do with emotional life. Cognitive intelligence has received an enormous amount of attention whereas emotional intelligence very little so perhaps a comment on the former is necessary. Some decades ago IQ tests were widely used to predict an individual's success as they were thought to test an innate and fixed ability.

As a young teacher in England I administered IQ tests in the 11+ exams using Moray House tests based on standardised Stanford-Binet Tests. Having passed 20% of the pupils into Grammar Schools and put the other 80% into Secondary Modern who left school at 15 with no exams they became a self-fulfilling prophecy. To be brief, the Grammar School leavers were more successful than the others and the high correlation validated the tests. When I came to Scotland in 1962 I was engaged in the campaigns to change the system of Junior and Senior Secondaries into Comprehensive Schools. Many studies have now shown that IQ contributes, at best, 20% to the factors that contribute to success in life. Daniel Goldman's concern is with a key set of other characteristics he calls emotional intelligence.

As you will have already guessed, the best predictor of success in our particular society is social class but this, in itself, is multi-factorial especially when we discuss expectation and motivation in particular economic and cultural systems. The Intelligence tests were then renamed Verbal Reasoning tests. Similarly, it seems to me, that individual emotions are responding to a particular cultural environment or society and perhaps we should go a step further than Goleman and study the interaction of the two rather than thinking of emotions as mere individual attributes in an individualistic society such as the U.S. if we are to assess their use value in particular circumstances and vicissitudes of life.

That aside and having disposed of the notion of intelligence as fixed and innate, it allowed people to turn their attention to the role of emotions in cognitive acts. That is, psychologists turned to how rationality is guided by feeling. Goleman quotes Gardner that the core of interpersonal intelligence includes the capacities to discern and respond appropriately to the moods, temperaments, motivations and desires of other people - the key to self knowledge.

I If intelligence and emotions are not mutually exclusive Goleman turns to the question, “Can emotions be intelligent?” and presents five main domains:

1. Knowing one's emotions

2. Managing emotions

3. Motivating oneself

4. Recognising emotions in others

5. Handling relationships.

On Happiness

Especially interesting are the findings that "up to a per capita income level of $20,000 a year, as poor countries grow richer their inhabitants grow happier. Above this threshold, however, the correlation breaks down….." Yet those with obscene wealth aggressively strive for more. They don't need it but deny it to others and don't get any happier in the process. Why not?

There's a U.S. magazine which publishes the top ten richest individuals every year. One of them became terribly depressed and spread his misery around until one day his wife pressed him for an answer - he replied that he had dropped down to No.11! So, rather than search for Dave's "happiness", men (especially men) fight for status and power derived from wealth in a capitalist jungle - and the devil take the hindmost.

At the risk of oversimplifying the characteristics of human behaviour, this leads me to the question: if human beings only need to achieve a certain "comfort level" for an optimum state of happiness and socialist ideals and goals bring the most good to most people why are they so difficult to achieve? Is it not that individuals and societies are much more complex than we like to think and that in our efforts to make our appeals easier to understand we make rainbows black and white? All very obvious but I think we are deluded us into thinking that we know the answers. Therefore let me try and restate this "complexity" in the form of a hierarchy of eight aphorisms and remember that each one has already been described and explained in long bibliographies!

My aim is merely to indicate that we need to understand the human condition without which our search for a better world will remain "pie in the sky" as we continually fail to appreciate the strength of the forces at work within us, as well as within society at large. Complicated? Yes but this is a summary of the basics.

1. A human being is a biologically autonomous individual but is especially a **social animal,** and **civilised** as a result of historical, cultural, economic and environmental factors.

2. We have two built-in basic drives, **to survive and to procreate** from which are derived many emotional and behavioral characteristics; many "hardwired" from our evolutionary past as hunter-gatherers and others from a sophisticated upbringing and education.

3. What differentiates us from animals are our **language-based abilities** to imagine, think abstractly and argue rationally. Most importantly, these are inextricably mixed with our strong emotions and drives.

4. We are born to live as members of ever-widening groups from the family to communities but **unequal power relationships** lead **inevitably** to the seeds of conflict between and within groups.

5. Although conflicts of interest are **inevitable**; violence is **not.**

6. Those with **power, wealth and privilege** always strive to retain them but there are no simple solutions to changing the resultant social, economic and political structures towards the betterment of the majority.

7. The tempering of anger, frustration, misery and aggression arising out of social injustice depends on the availability of dialogue and an appreciation of the inherent contradictions, attitudes and behavior of those involved. The resolution of problems and tensions requires a participatory and not merely a representative democratic structure.

8. We consequently make mistakes in our attempts to organize society, e.g.:

a) the **liberal** fallacy that focusses **only** on attitudes: (trying to be nice to everybody/ being all things to all men/playing for popularity etc.).

b) the **conservative** fallacy that putting a lid on conflict to maintain the status quo is sustainable: (thus sacrificing the long-term for short term gain).

c) the **marxist** fallacy that resolving class conflict **alone**, will inevitably lead to a better society: (neither will ignoring the class struggle, allowing market fundamentalism to dominate decision-making, while, at the same time, paying lip-service to reduce social injustice - Blairism?

On the relevance of Marxism

Preamble

Many people have claimed to be Marxists including myself have read little of Marx in the original. This is not surprising as there now exists over 50 volumes of his writings, each of 800 pages! More importantly, bits have been selected, embroidered and dogmatically used and Marx himself commented on reading one review by saying, "If that's Marxism then I'm not a Marxist!" The question for us is: "Has his philosophy any relevance today?"

I'll make free use of Terry Eagleton's Chapter on Marx in *The Great Philosophers* edited by Monk and *Why Read Marx Today* by Jonathan Wolff and you can make your own mind up.

Background

Marx, a jew, was born in the Rhineland of Prussia in 1818. His lawyer father was converted to Christianity when the authorities made him choose between his job and his religion. Marx was a brilliant student and for his PhD compared the 2 Greek philosophers Democratus and Epicurus. He failed to get an academic job because he was declared an atheist and a radical so he turned to journalism. His anti-government writing then forced him to move to Paris, then to Brussels and finally to London with his wife and children where he wrote his masterpiece *"Capital"*.

On Religion

His economic analysis has been the most influential and his study of capitalism still stands but here we are concerned with his underlying philosophy. The younger Marx was immersed in German philosophy which, at the time, was dominated by that of Hegel and he was surrounded by the "Young Hegelians", a radical group attempting to answer the question, why did God bother to create a world so full of misery and suffering? Hegel's answer was that God simply would not be God without the world to rule, and a ruler needs to encounter 'the other' if he is to understand how to rule.

Following work by David Strauss and Bruno Bauer, the Young Hegelians concluded that Christianity is simply an illusion but Marx was dissatisfied with this as an answer. "But why did it catch on so well?" he asked. Feuerbach argued that the reason why human beings resembled God, is not that God created us in his image, but that we created him in ours. However, Marx, was not content with this either and believed it to be rather superficial because it did not address the cause. Briefly, Marx argued that human beings invented religion because their life on earth was so miserable and uncertain. They needed comforting and made his famous remark: "Religion is the opium of the people." He therefore deemed it necessary to remove the causes, of which exploitation and alienation are basic. It therefore cannot simply be suppressed or banned to make it disappear.

Alienation

We may agree what is meant by exploitation but what is alienation? Alienation arises from our attempts to create a world we don't properly understand and have become strangers to it. We are now dominated and often mystified by the products of our hand and brain in a market economy. We have become merely consumers without a satisfying life-style. Marx explains this key point of his philosophy that alienation "is an objective fact about our lives... that two things which belong together come apart... and the human essence becomes detached from human existence." Belief in the supernatural is one form of alienation but Marx concentrated on labour alienation especially production line technology. Work under capitalism, he describes, involves no self-fulfilment and with the normal 12-hour day at the time there was little opportunity to get involved in the family, community and constructive leisure time. We are made to want things and not our real needs. That is, under capitalism we become, as Marx said, "Alienated from our species-essence… The human essence of nature exists only for **social** man; for only here does nature exist for him as a bond with other men, as his existence for others and their existence for him, as the vital element of human reality; only here does it exist as the basis of his own human existence... Society is therefore the perfected unity in essence of man with nature… It is above all necessary to avoid once more establishing 'society' as an abstraction over and against the individual. The individual **is** the social being..." We are still discussing these 150 years later and, alas, we are now dominated by the American values of individualism, money, and power over others, not as just a market tool but as a way of life and alienation is as strong as ever.

Historical Materialism

Why was Marx sceptical of philosophers? He gave the short answer in his well-known edict that "philosophers have only interpreted the world in various ways; the point, however, is to change it." This requires a new self-understanding but to know oneself in a new way is to alter ourselves. Moreover, to seek to emancipate oneself involves questions of value so the usual distinction made in philosophy between facts and values becomes blurred. Marx's criticism of German philosophy lay in its idealist base, seeing consciousness as the foundation of reality. He stated that "The production of ideas, of conceptions, of consciousness, is at first directly woven with the material activity and the material intercourse of men, the language of real life… they are conditioned by a definite development of their productive forces…" Elsewhere he continued, "It is not the consciousness of men that determines their being, but their social being that determines their consciousness," and later he explains how, in changing the world we change ourselves.

Surprising to some he talked a lot about freedom. Freedom is possible, he explains, only when our needs have been satisfied; that is, freedom from want, disease, fear and superstition and not the neo-liberal freedom of an individual to exploit his fellow man (and perhaps he should have added "and nature" but no-one at the time did!). Unfortunately, language can block as well as facilitate communication. "Language is as old as consciousness," he said, "language is practical real consciousness that exists for other men as well and, therefore, it also exists for me... and only arises from the need of intercourse with other men." Notice that he follows the normal practice of the time of masculine terminology. Both language and consciousness exist because they have a social and survival function as Darwinists have explained.

For Marx, the derived culture has only one parent and that is labour. In a family and tribal society it is cooperative. In a slave, feudal or capitalist society labour is exploited in a power relationship of the haves and have-nots, and there is inevitable class conflict. Our thinking is accordingly conditional on its historical and social context; especially our relationship to the means of production. For instance, there could not have been any Marxism in Greek or in Feudal times. Marxism is a product of the very epoch it desires to move beyond. It is a guide to action and not a prescription. Eagleton remarks that, "It is darkly ironic that his own work would, among other things, give birth in time to just such sterile system-building."

However, Marx was neither a dreamer nor a Utopian but neither was he a mechanical materialist like Thomas Hobbes. His work was based on what he and Engels called historical materialism. Marx's point was that if key theoretical problems have their anchorage in the reality of social contradictions, then they can only be politically rather than philosophically resolved and this culminated in the Communist Manifesto. I'll quote only one paragraph in order that you may appreciate why so many generations in the last 150 years have been inspired to search for a socialist alternative to capitalism.

"Capitalism has replaced feudalism," Marx explains, "and has drowned the most heavenly ecstasies of religious fervour, of chivalrous enthusiasm, of philistine sentimentalism, in the icy water of egotistical calculation... In one word, for exploitation, veiled by religious and political illusions; it has substituted naked, shameless, direct, brutal exploitation... It has torn away from the family its sentimental veil, and has reduced the family relation to a mere money relation... the bourgoisie cannot exist without constantly revolutionizing the instruments of production, and thereby the relations of production, and with them the whole relations of society... Constant revolutions of production, uninterrupted disturbance of all social conditions, everlasting uncertainty and agitation distinguish the bourgoise epoch from all earlier ones. All fixed, fast-frozen relations, with their train of ancient and venerable prejudices and opinions, are swept away, all new-formed ones become antiquated before they can ossify. All that is solid melts into air; all that is holy is profaned, and man is at last compelled to face with sober senses, his real conditions of life and his relations with his kind."

My own thoughts

The philosophy of Marx was further developed by his lifetime collaborator Engels especially on the evolution of society, the laws of the transformation of quantity into quality and of the dialectical interaction of man and his social and physical environment mediated by consciousness. I think it is of interest that the use to which Marxism has been put has varied with time and space but especially with different cultures. In the less developed world it has led to dogmatism in the Soviet Union, the cult of the personality in North Korea, revisionism in Vietnam and South Africa and pragmatism in China, Cuba, Kerala and Angola; all of them in the face of the hostile developed capitalist west. I am not, however, much taken by 'isms' and in Europe Marxists have tried to articulate their ideas through currently accepted philosophies with a revival of interest in Hegel, existentialism, structuralism, Freud and the work of academics such as Althusser, Adorno, Marcuse and Habermas. I think Marx would have attacked much of the latter saying as he did that "the dispute over the reality or non-reality of thinking that is isolated from practice is a purely scholastic question" and of limited significance. In contrast, he might have approved of the eurocommunist revision based on the writings of the Italian

Gramsci. The present trend for Marxists in the struggle to change society is inspired with the complexity of ecological, feminist and pluralist perspectives and is by no means dead.

The Future

The abundant works of Marx have little to say about the future state of society. However, he distinguished between the rights of a citizen in a liberal democracy (freedom to ...) and the rights of man as a social being (freedom from ...) as already mentioned. He declared that only socialism could end the exploitation of man by man, so the key issue then is to change society for the better, knowing that those who gain wealth, privilege and power from the present system naturally wish to perpetuate it and are therefore intent on eradicating Marxism from the agenda. On the other hand, those who wish to change society must face the facts of what is usually described as human nature. We have self-awareness, foresight, judgement and choice. We have the capacity for moral scrutiny but to be moral we must also realize how thoroughly we are not. Kenan Malik (author of *Man Beast and Zombie*) goes further and says that evolution has designed "new ways of monitoring our own thoughts and keeping track of them. Such access to our thinking is what we experience as consciousness... The development of consciousness, and hence of freedom, requires humans, through historical progress, to begin to control nature and to regulate its impact on our lives... freedom," he said, "is a political, not a scientific, issue." I think there are few words in the English language that have been so much abused as "freedom", "democracy" and communism, especially in the context of aggressive market fundamentalism.

Yes, I agree with Marx that human affairs are essentially historically and culturally based and therefore not represented by the universality and precision of the sciences. Human affairs are set in the context of the overall progressive sweep of history but our thinking not only depends on our position in a changing global culture but also on searching inwards as well as outwards for answers. There are patterns to discern in both but they are surely far too complicated to have any of the predictability that Marx had hoped for. But as Professor Wolff concludes, "Marx remains the most profound and acute critic of capitalism, even as it exists today. We may have no confidence in his solutions to the problems he identifies, but this does not make the problems go away."

Finally may I quote Walpole who said that life is a comedy for those who think and a tragedy for those who feel.

I think that the human condition is both but it's what you think is what matters!

On Sartre's Freedom

We are condemned to be Free!

Freedom has exercised the minds as of many great thinkers. I looked it up in the Oxford Companion to Philosophy and here is the list. Freedom and determinism, libertarianism autonomy, the four- freedoms of the United Nations Charter, Freedom of speech, freedom from hunger, freedom from fear, freedom from suffering and disease, freedom of goodness and reason, self determination, right to a homeland, freedom to assemble and disassemble and so on. Note that these are freedoms **from** and not freedom **to**, for example freedom to exploit the earth and its peoples to satisfy our selfish desires with the ideology of the free market which is so characteristic of today's emphasis on individual choice irrespective of our responsibility to others.

The extent of man's liberty to choose to live as he desires must be weighed against the claims of many other values, of which quality, justice, happiness, security, or public order are perhaps the most obvious examples. For this reason it cannot be unlimited. We are reminded that the liberty of the strong, whether their strength is physical or economic, must be restrained. That we cannot have everything, is a necessary, not a contingent, truth.

Sartre, however, takes issue with this kind of thinking that some of our actions are free whereas others are determined. He denies that causality operates upon human behaviour. He illustrates his ideas with a simple story of a hiker who has been overcome with fatigue so that he acted as he had to do, or has he freely chosen to rest? HOW are we to decide this question?

Sartre believed that human actions always needed to be understood by it's reference to both objective and subjective features. He argues that all actions have two causes, one external and one internal which we can call the motive. Sartre says that neither the hiker's subjective state that being thirsty, nor the objective situation, there being a drink in the fridge, are sufficient to motivate his action in order for him to act. He must now annihilate his thirst, that is, he must transcend it and he can choose to do so.

On Creating a Peaceful World

No Quick Fixes to Creating a Peaceful World by Non-violent Means

On 6 June 1944 the Allied invasion against the Nazi armies started in Normandy. I was a seventeen-year-old Merchant Navy cadet on a ship in the Belgian Congo bringing back copper, palm oil, rubber and mahogany with the Atlantic convoys. Then, after the nazis were defeated, we heard on the ship's news bulletin that the Americans had destroyed Hiroshima and Nagasaki with nuclear weapons to demonstrate their overwhelming power to Japan and the rest of the world. In consequence, I reacted fervently into a "never again" mode of thinking, reading, listening and campaigning for a world free of nuclear weapons in a non-sectarian way. But in the Cold War hysteria that followed how could I be right and the government and media wrong?

Gandhi said that "the claim to infallibility on the part of a human being would be untenable… This, however, does not leave us without any guidance whatsoever. The sum-total of the experience of the world is available and would be for all time to come. Moreover, there are not many fundamental truths. There is only one… otherwise known as non-violence." However, it seems to me that convincing enough individuals of non-violence until there is a working majority in agreement would take an unacceptably long time. How then could a policy of non-violence be made effective in achieving the resolution of disputes? Let me start by running through a series of aphorisms, each of which requires a detailed discussion in itself, but may help our understanding of the overall picture of what it means to be human and we can then move quickly to the more important end product.

Man is biologically an autonomous individual with two basic drives, namely to survive and to procreate with many derived emotional and behavioural characteristics. For example, his greed and aggression, especially male, are legacies from his hunter-gathering gene pool but he is also a social animal living most of the time co-operating in families, workplaces and communities. We should therefore look at "human nature" as a complex interaction between genetic inheritance and social influences. Even more important is man's socially induced ability to communicate by abstract symbolic language enabling him to imagine and create new worlds for himself; thus differentiating himself from the rest of the animal kingdom yet organically connected to it.

From this supreme ability arises his wonderful and inspiring human spirit, but in saying this it is easy to forget the built-in legacies from his evolved past. As Gandhi said, "The spirit in me pulls one way, the flesh in me pulls in the opposite direction."

It was therefore a long struggle before Gandhi focused on the key element of non-violent mass action against apartheid and colonialism. His great achievement was to reject the perceived assumptions of the day that the British Empire was unchallengeable because of its overwhelming military, economic and political power. However, he demonstrated that this power is impotent in the face of a substantial proportion of the population who are prepared to withhold their cooperation and suffer the violence that is initially made against them. The British found that military action against a defenseless population appalled the rest of the world yet they were trained to act in no other way. Military force could not compel obedience and eventually had to quit. Is not the United States also vulnerable if it continues to assume that might is right?

So, to repeat and emphasize two points.

1. Our ability to think rationally about our objectives for a peaceful world is inextricably mixed with complex drives and emotions including aggressive actions.

2. Non-violent mass action can be effective.

This is important as we now have the capability and choice to destroy ourselves and other life on our planet or to build a peace culture that would, in political terms, make such destruction to be seen as counterproductive by those who wish is to perpetrate it. Let us not be naïve in this. Conflicts between individuals and group interests are endemic and ubiquitous. For example, imagine you are travelling across a town by the different modes of transport, on foot, by cycle, car and bus. Anger bubbles up as a pedestrian vilifies the car driver, as the car driver riles against the cyclist, as a cyclist shakes his fist against the bus driver and so on but in our different roles we also recognise that violence is not the answer to our problems. However, these conflicts and contradictions of role change are transient and trivial compared to other and more important issues at stake. We cannot change our role if we consider skin colour, social class, gender, culture, history and genetic make-up.

Conflicts of interest on a global scale, say between nations, multinational companies, religious, racial and social classes have tremendous impact and are inevitable **but violence is not inevitable**. This is the great lesson to be learnt. Conflict, then, is about fear of another's intentions with the attendant dilemmas, problems and disputes. More to the point, however, unequal power relationships lead to exploitation by the privileged party and the seeds of conflict and violence can easily arise. The degree of anger, frustration and aggression depend on the depth and projection of contradiction, attitude and behaviour. If violence breaks out it will escalate unless conflict resolution measures are involved. **Violence begets violence.** Revenge is sweet. Revenge is powerful. Revenge is a motive knowing no solution except death and destruction. As Gandhi said, "An eye for an eye will leave the whole world blind". The limited vision of those states and ideologues able to identify only the act of violence and not its roots, perpetuate the very acts they seek to condemn and so the spiral of violence continues.

I therefore take a pragmatic rather than a religious view as worthy of consideration but what kind of violence are we talking about? Professor of Peace Studies, Johan Galtung asks us to look deeper into several kinds of violence. For example, there is hidden violence that may be causing the more obvious forms of physical violence such as slavery, where slaves may be passive but under a continual threat of violence. Slavery is also structural violence like apartheid, colonialism and the exploitation of cheap labour where there is no protection or defense of the workers. Galtung therefore goes beyond physical violence and includes many other forms with a very broad definition that violence is anything which prevents a person fulfilling his or her full potential. For example, he includes emotional violence of anger, fear, frustration, irritation, stress, fatigue and sleep loss, leading to insults, the denial of dignity, self-esteem and psychological violence. We also see conformity violence on our television screens when groups of young men are engaged in street fighting perhaps after binge drinking or a football match which some liken to a reversion to tribalism. Man's inhumanity to man is perhaps seen as particularly wretched in the phenomenon of child soldiers, as in Africa, where the influence of their elders is at a formative age when social pressures can be decisive in permanently warping their lifestyles. Lastly, a relatively few people, and it is only a few, have a psychopathic personality with violence they are unable to control but this can be acquired as well as genetically induced, and it may well be best for the community for them to be institutionalized if rehabilitation is not possible.

Thus the word violence is an umbrella term. It is therefore inadequate to merely call for a non-violent resolution to disputes without the identification and analysis of the causes and circumstances. **There are no quick fixes** even if the media demands them, but there is another necessary ingredient that **Trust begets Trust** - the basis of any relationship but not necessarily easy when two parties are fearful of each other. It has been found that people and those in power are better able to discuss a root problem when trust has been built up and when they believe there is a non-violent solution. This takes time, expertise and patience.

Crucially, according to United Nations negotiators, if constructive dialogue is going to be successful then attitudes and behaviour are likely to have changed. However mistakes have been made in the past in attempting conflict resolution when the focus has been solely on one aspect such as history or attitude or behaviour or by imposing a temporary solution from outside and leaving it to fester without lancing the boil. Experience suggests that it is fallacious to rely only on one aspect alone and especially on goodwill or platitudes or the non-committal responses of those involved. On the other hand goodwill, like trust, is vitally necessary if the problem is to be examined with a view to a permanent solution.

We must therefore move on, with the accumulated post-Second World War experience, with situations in which conflicts are now potentially violent but are more varied, complex and technologically lethal. On the other hand, electronic communication, experience and knowledge of non-violent means of settling disputes are more easily available now but whether mankind has yet acquired enough collective wisdom to use them is doubtful! We should also remind ourselves that nation states were not created to work for world peace and justice but to further their self-interests as defined by their elites. The only effective instrument on a global scale for peacemaking, peace keeping and especially peace building and empowerment is the United Nations. Yes! UNO needs to be reformed and improved but we should be aware that there are those who wish to oppose or sideline the UN but in a more subtle way than open opposition, prefer to use these problems of updating as excuses for procrastination. Again the focus of the United Nations has previously been on conflicts *between* states. Now most conflicts are occurring *within* states. The international community has the responsibility of seeking solutions but there is always the danger of outside intervention with ulterior motives. States, other than those in dispute, often have at their own at agenda and propose UN resolutions accordingly, with the danger of multiplying rather than solving the problems. We can all name examples, especially in the Middle East.

The major player in the world today is, of course, the United States. Its military, economic and cultural dominance is so overwhelming that many are pessimistic about the possibilities of achieving world peace. If another

Gandhi emerged today he would see a completely different South Africa and India. He would now see a European continent which, for the first time in history, cannot envisage conflicts being solved by violent means. On the other hand, in this new century of ours, we have a vastly different world of globalisation, uncertainty, individualism and market fundamentalism with, for example, 780 American military bases, many small but some very large in three quarters of the world's nation states, supposedly to defend the economic and political interests of the United States even though it seems to an increasing number of observers that its actions are increasingly counterproductive.

So we can now return to the vulnerability of even the most powerful military forces in the face of non-violent mass action. Our conclusion should therefore be to give priority to the development of a peace culture using as many ways as possible, with as many sections of the community as possible. This cannot be left to governments and the representatives we elect every few years. People should be educated to think of peace, not merely as the absence of war but as their self-fulfillment as human beings and mobilised accordingly. Civil society and non-governmental organisations, as well as individuals with expertise can be rallied to urge governments to act, whether this is from a principled or expedient perspective. As individuals we have a decisive role to play. Participation by all concerned is the name of the game. Remember that those with power and privilege look to the military to defend their interests. The situation therefore demands an end to all sectarianism with an awareness of the strength of opposing vested interests in order to formulate policies for effective action. Finally, we have the immediate responsibility to exert our power on our own Government, and because of its special relationship, to urge the government to convince the United States that it is in their long-term enlightened self-interest to seek non-violent solutions.

We return to where we began by repeating that conflicts are inevitable but violence is not. By example and with united, concerted non-violent action and argument we can make peacemaking, peace building, peacekeeping and reconciliation the norm of human relations rather than wishful thinking and pious hopes. As individuals we should assert our own power in this aspiration. At grassroots level we should be encouraged by the depth of present feeling in the world today, the increase in non-violent demonstrations, the softening of boundaries within humankind and the widening of international solidarity of non-governmental organisations. A peace culture is growing, perhaps not fast enough, but the opportunity is there. It is up to each one of us to seize on that opportunity.

On Cuba

Cuba is a poor country, yet has made remarkable progress in health, education and the reduction of poverty since the revolution. James Wolfenson, President of the World Bank, acknowledges that "they should be congratulated on what they have done" (Lobe 2001). It is therefore difficult to understand why this socialist-oriented Island continues to be ignored in the many publications on a global poverty and those barriers to human development in much of the world requires massive help from outside.

Cuba - A Revolution in Motion - Isaac Saney Zed Books is a comprehensive introduction to all aspects of Cuban life is therefore a breath of fresh air by this Canadian academic. It is really a text book with an extensive bibliography and index but is surprisingly easy to read. Saney provides a most impressive sweep of the dynamics of survival and change over the last decade since the total collapse of Soviet support and the intensification of the United States' efforts to change its regime by all means short of invasion.

I found the analysis of Cuba's governance and the economic, social and political institutions particularly interesting. Welcome too are the descriptions of what is happening at community level with a bottom-up electoral system. More importantly, perhaps, he details the present generational transition and transfer of power with current changes and adaptation to circumstances. He analyses the political developments and what will happen when Castro dies.

Saney's deep knowledge and understanding of the dynamics of Cuba also leads him to pose relevant questions, show some weaknesses and critically examine certain aspects such as capital punishment, the dollar/peso inequalities and Agricultural Policies. However, the cost of organising a welfare state with an emphasis on education and health and the removal of the poverty we see elsewhere may not fit easily into our world of market fundamentalism and Cuba will remain isolated and threatened.

Cuba is therefore not a model that can or should be exported as a package but we can learn some fundamental aspects from the debate surrounding the conditions and instrumentalities necessary to achieve a higher quality of life in developing countries. One aspect is the active participation at grassroots level especially of women, integrated into a hierarchy of power structures such that, for instance, the natural disasters wrought by an increasing number of hurricanes have been successfully managed with a remarkably low death-rate, especially compared with the rest of the Caribbean.

On Kerala

It was a great holiday as well as an amazing example of the importance how a communist administration put the education of women as an urgent priority and how the Congress Party did all it could to defeat it but the legacy stays. Thank goodness!

***KERALA - The Development Experience.* Edited by G.Paraytil. Zed Books. £15.99 -** was reviewed below after a study visit in 2006.

Kerala is the south west province of India and the Master of Trinity College, Cambridge, an authority on South-East Asia, Amartya Sen, wrote, "Despite the fact that the economic growth in Kerala has been slow... it has achieved tremendous results in important areas such as literacy, life expectancy and mortality rates. The Indian government should try to emulate the Kerala experience."

Consider, for example the following extracts from the statistics for the 1990's (page 18):

Average Income - Kerala $324; India as a whole $390; USA $28,740.

Female literacy - Kerala 87%; India 38%; USA 96%

Infant Mortality per 1000 - Kerala 13; India 65; USA 7

Birth Rate per 1000 – Kerala 18; India 29; USA 16

Of the less developed countries only Sri Lanka and Cuba compare with Kerala's high status of women. Now compare Kerala with the prospects for the nearby province of Andhra Pradesh whose Chief Minister Naidu has invited the World Bank, foreign investors and Clare Short's Development Department to finance the factories and the industrialisation of agriculture in huge farm consolidations which will put 20 million off the land into shanty towns of plastic and cardboard in order to supply the USA and Israel with cheap fruit, vegetables and flowers. Katharine Ainger of the *New Internationalist* says that the World Bank proposes that welfare be reduced and the money spent on the infrastructure. The peasant farmers are protesting but being ignored. When we read today that the Indian government says it wants to reduce the 270 million in India outside Kerala who go to bed without having eaten all day because they cannot afford the available food we realise the scale of the problem. At the same time the Indian government is encouraging other provinces to follow Andrha Pradesh's example and not that of Kerala. Ainger concludes, "If there is to be an alternative vision it will have to come from the opposite direction - that is not from the top down but from the ground up."

This is where the significance of the Kerala model seems to have gone unnoticed except by this book which gives Kerala's answers through a series of easily read academic papers arising out of recent conferences. The background of historical and cultural ingredients is described and includes its seaboard location, the spice trade, European missionaries and the religious tolerance of the 30 million population and mix of 60% Hindu. 20% Christian and 20% Muslim. Deemed to be more significant are the 20th. century struggles against caste and class privilege, a matrilineal sub-group with property rights for women, a high density rural population with a participatory civic society and well-organised trades unions and political parties. Although this provides fertile ground it does not fully explain why the changes to more equality and social justice have taken place so rapidly during the last 50 years of independence when only Kerala "took off" leaving the rest of India behind. It certainly wasn't any economic advantage so what was it?

When the province of Kerala was formed the ruling Maharajas were sidelined and the first elections in 1957 brought in a communist government arising out of their strong base at grass roots level, as exemplified by their recruitment of 370,000 volunteers in a mass literacy campaign. Government land reform which dispossessed absentee landlords, a minimum wage, investment in health, education, poverty alleviation and devolution of power to village leveled particularly to the rise in the status of women and this had a multiplier effect. The **reduction in the gender and poverty gaps was instrumental in the changes that rapidly followed**. However, the communist government was removed from office by Central Government for exceeding its remit and since then the dominant CPI (Marxist) has exerted its influence through a left alliance. There have since been two coalitions alternating, viz. the Communist and left Alliance and the Congress Party and Muslim Alliance but community involvement and compromise solutions from the bottom up have remained strong and red flags fly everywhere from villages to tea plantations reflecting the ongoing political debate. **It is a participatory and not merely our kind of representative democracy.**

Western governments and power centres promote development in terms of economic growth and industrial investment using cheap labour within a globally-organised free market system imposing a reduction in public expenditure through structural adjustment. Even NGOs have been infected with the same ideology on the basis of "there is no alternative". However, disillusion with the neo-liberal development nostrums is increasing everywhere and this scholarly work by eminent social scientists shows how a nation can pull itself up by its own bootstraps given the political will, fewer corrupt and career politicians and a vibrant grass-roots activism.

Of course, Kerala is not insulated from the effects of globalisation and two major questions are posed. How can Kerala's present economic problems be resolved and is the Kerala model sustainable and replicable elsewhere? There are no easy answers but the detailed arguments, facts, examples and statistics of Kerala's complex development cogently presented in 274 pages, will give inspiration to all those interested in learning how to adapt the lessons of Kerala to the global millions in dire poverty, disease, ignorance and misery. It breathes the necessary optimism that we ourselves can live in a better world.

On Scottish Independence

Some of the letters to the Scotsman on the Independence Referendum 2014 in reply to feature articles.

Ray Newton. December 2012

Scotsman

"I think there is a general misunderstanding about the Independence Referendum. A 'Yes' vote would only give the Scottish Government a mandate to negotiate an agreement with the UK Government. The 'Yes' campaign must present a list of desirable objectives before the referendum in October 2014. Afterwards negotiations would take for at least two years and because there is a big majority in Scotland for the removal of nuclear weapons the Scottish Government could stand firm. Other issues like currency might take ten years depending on the strength of feeling. It is also possible that Scottish Labour will divorce its 'big middle-of-the-road brother' in London, take a much more radical line especially on tax and regulation and be voted into office, perhaps as a coalition with the Greens and complete the deal. In other words, all things are possible if we have the will to govern ourselves."

Scotsman

At present Labour is to the right of the SNP but things would change radically if Scottish members of the Labour Party followed the scenario of the former First Minister McLeish instead of that imposed by its London HQ. Scottish Labour should reject the Anglo-American model of an unregulated free-market, a banking system of greed, a widening gap between rich and poor and the threat of nuclear weapons. A campaign on these issues could end the present malaise and cynicism and gain a Labour majority in the next parliament to complete the independence negotiations in 2016 as a global example of a Change for the better. What a marvelous prospect that would be!

Scotsman

For too long we have been made to admire the rich and privileged instead of the working people. That is the significance of Danny Boyle's Olympic salute to the British people and is echoed in the independence debate. The 'No Vote' campaign is negative, trivial, mudslinging and conservative whereas the 'Yes Vote' invites us to strive together for a more sharing and caring society instead of the individualism and greed prioritised by our imperialist-minded English neighbour. The issue is not about breaking up the UK but about asserting our right to decide our own future, following the different path of traditional Scottish values of equality, fairness and community. This means renegotiating the Treaty of Union over NATO, currency, taxation, the Queen and Commonwealth, oil, public funding and crucially Trident, sending a message to the rest of the world that there are more important values than military dominance and market fundamentalism - in other words, Danny Boyle's vision of human progress.

Scotland on Sunday

As a Green Party member I think that Maria Fyfe's letter (22 July) under "Independence: more questions than answers" shows that the Unionist campaign is merely a conservative one of no change and quite negative. It actually confirms its opposite - the need for two years of debate on the referendum and then two more of negotiations on home rule and interdependence. As politics is the art of the possible there are both priorities and longer-term issues. Now is the time for the Scottish people to take the responsibility for their own different future instead of it being decided by an imperialist-minded neighbour. That is especially the case for the nuclear issue where the overwhelming majority in Scotland do not want the very expensive, dangerous and useless Trident.

More importantly, as my Labour MSP Sarah Boyack told me (19 June), "If we were NOT to replace Trident it would send a powerful message internationally, potentially a very positive move in multinational disarmament." It would break the log jam in negotiating global nuclear disarmament as promised to those signing the non-nuclear weapons commitment.

What a prize that would be for the world's 7 billion people! Scotland's reputation would make us far safer, joining the vast majority of influential small independent countries. That is the real significance of a Yes vote.

Scotsman

According to the polls most people in Scotland would agree with Bruce Skivington (letters 12 July) that Scotland does not need Trident and its massive waste of financial resources, "as there is little antagonism in the world towards Scotland." The issue of independence is therefore crucial. The military know that nuclear weapons can never be used but the UK Government uses Trident to keep its seat on the Security Council and close to America's attempted global control.

This disastrous and counterproductive imperialist policy leads to terrorist reaction to the extent that the UK is now putting anti-aircraft missiles on the top of London flats! Scotland, however, has a chance to determine its own future. For instance, my Labour MSP Sarah Boyack was one of the majority in the Scottish Parliament who voted against nuclear weapons and states (June 2012), "If we were NOT to replace Trident it would send a powerful message internationally, potentially a very positive move in multilateral disarmament negotiations with other countries." However, what she failed to say is that this can only be achieved with a vote for independence and not by joining the very conservative NO campaign.

A POLITICAL DIALOGUE

Scotsman

As usual, Joyce MacMillan gets to the fundamentals of politics. She is right to point out (8 June) that Ed Miliband and the Labour Party are "still weighed down with Blair baggage" which included cosying-up to the rich with neoliberal economics, foreign intervention and Trident first-strike nuclear capability. This might get more votes in the English Marginals but such a policy fails in Scotland and is far to the right of the SNP, hence fewer Labour MSPs. Their only way forward as a political party is to become independent from UK Labour and, like the Scottish Green Party, help the people of Scotland to decide their own future. After a successful 'Yes vote' they can then join the complex negotiations with the imperialist Westminster Government for Scotland as a self-governing state in 2016. The resulting increase in political participation will release the energy and imagination that will make Scotland an influential global leader amongst the many small countries in the United Nations to a more secure world.

Scotsman 29 January 2013

Dr. McCormick asks (28 Jan.), "What would be the benefits of an independent Scotland unilaterally banning the continued presence of our current (Trident) weapons system?" Firstly, it would remove Scotland as a target. Secondly, it would trigger negotiations for global nuclear disarmament which the nuclear weapon powers declared they would do if the non-nuclear countries signed the Non-Proliferation Treaty. However, the UK and the USA have gone back on their promise and hesitated taking the initiative. Thirdly, it would release the highly skilled workers that are so urgently in demand elsewhere as in the oil industry and fourthly, it would release the thirty billion pounds earmarked to be spent on replacing this white elephant, continuing the fear it engenders over its declared first use against the dissolved enemy of the U.S.S.R. Lastly, I was pleased at Lesley Riddoch's reference (Perspectives 28 January) to Labour's former defense minister, Des Browne, saying that nuclear deterrence as a cornerstone of defense strategy was "decreasingly effective and increasingly risky". Only independence can start the ball rolling.

Ray Newton

On the Voice or Darfur Woman

Absent from Eric's close questioning is the role of women in the community of work, leisure and politics. This is a global issue requiring an emphasis on the education of girls and women and I am proud to have been involved in supporting women's campaigns especially in Sudan.

As the **Founder, Tutor and Donor** of The Voice of Darfur Women in London I am pleased to say that it is now well established and expanding its influence together with its close partner, Sudanese Mothers for Peace and Develpment in Khartoum, - planting the seeds of feminism at the start of a long and hard road for the empowerment of Darfur women which requires the understanding and support of men in their own interest.

The Voice of Darfur Women

Chairperson: Dr. Mariam Suliman. 16 Mouldsford House, Rowstock Gardens, London N7 0BE.

marioma89@yahoo.com

Secretary: Asia Lessan. Treasurer: Ekhlas Ahmed. Registered Charity 1143308

Adviser: Ray Newton, newton@raypat.plus.com

Darfur?

What's the problem?

Why is there a crisis?

The history and culture of Darfur is the key to its present crisis. It is complex but the nomadic Arabs (Janjaweed) lived peacefully alongside the African farmers for hundreds of years so why is it such a violent place now? Climate chaos, rising population and expectations, the handing over of power by the British to a small minority of educated Arabs, the undemocratic coup by El Bashir in 1989 and his refusal to share power and resources with the people of Darfur led to violence and ethnic cleansing breaking out in 2003 and is continuing today with only a slow growth in UN peacekeepers.

A POLITICAL DIALOGUE

20,000 villages have been devastated, nearly one quarter of a million killed and the displacement of three million, mainly women and children, who have survived only by international aid. International pressure, especially by the United Nations, on the Government of Sudan will eventually lead to a negotiated and lasting peace leading to the return of the displaced people and postwar reconstruction of communities. But things will never be the same again. The refugees are a proud and self-reliant people. Their villages have been destroyed, families traumatised and communities damaged but their despair can be changed to HOPE by our trained, skilled and professional Sudanese women from the diaspora **in the UK.**

80% of the displaced persons are women who traditionally do most of the work in the home, the fields and the market place and also search for wood and water yet all decisions are made by the men. However, their experiences are leading to new thinking about their future role, but ignorance persists which must be removed.

All studies of development in poor countries have shown that the awareness, education, empowerment and status of women is crucial in the ongoing social, economic and political development but they need the help of our volunteers to point the way ahead.

The Voice of Darfur Women

Second Khartoum visit, Nov – Dec 2010

Report by Ekhlas Ahmed

Purpose:

1. To evaluate the first visit by Zeinab Burma and Maimona Ismali 22 July to 19 August 2010;

2. To give further courses in women's empowerment to the three founding groups of Darfuri women;

3. To start business plans to make and sell garments with sewing machines donated by an anonymous lady pensioner in Edinburgh in order to generate income for the groups.

We are now committed to the last year of a 3-year plan in association with our partners, "The Sudanese Mothers for Peace and Development" in Khartoum, sending them our trained volunteers twice a year for a month at a time to three groups of internally-displaced Darfuri women. We have already started the training, organising groups in Khartoum, El Geneina and El Fashir.

Enthusiastic Leaders have been elected but they need expert advice and ongoing help to form strong campaigning groups and networks for the rights of women to participate in the decision-making at all levels of society.

Bank account: VODW, Sort Code 206915, account 4317515

A Land Value Tax for Scotland

Fair, efficient and sustainable to replace Council Tax and Corporation Tax.

This is a one-page summary from a full and long report by Andy Wightman to the Scottish Green Party.

1. Owners of land can sit and do nothing but just wait for its value to rise because of change of use or upgrading of the surrounding area but then reap all the profits and pay no tax! The Government can easily get to know who owns the land, its classification, its assessed value (without the property on it) and with the new computerized air surveys, they know exactly the extent of every parcel, small or large. For instance, the European Community now pays millions of farmers a Common Agricultural Policy payment because, unlike formerly, they cannot be cheated with false land claims.

2. There have been several proposals in the past for such a tax but the land lobby of the richest owners has led to its rejection. Pilot studies of its feasibility have been made, e.g. Glasgow City Council in 2009 but more importantly, the British Labour Party in London which promotes the One Nation ideology does not wants it.

3. All land is classified from useless, grazing, forest, agricultural, commercial and industrial, residential etc. When, for instance, land is changed from agricultural use to residential its value immediately multiplies, as I was told was the case of the expansion of the village of Culloden resulting in a farmer making over a million without tax.

4. Social justice demands that the gains in land value be shared more

equitably with the community. It is not a tax on property but on the land according to its classification and <u>used accordingly</u>.

5. At present Speculators buy land and can 'sterilise' it for many years as 'land banks' e.g. Tesco has bought sites suitable for supermarkets but sold as separate parcels so rival supermarkets cannot be built there. Therefore, land classified as residential will be taxed at that rate. Farm land, if it not used will be taxed as farm land etc. Thus, the whole of society benefits from the optimum use of the land.

7. LVT is not a property tax. For instance, the cost of building a house does not vary much wherever it is built but the price of land is added to the building cost. The average cost of the plot in Scotland is £75,000 whereas in London it is £150,000 and Northern Ireland £40,000 so the cost to the client depends on the locality.

8. These are just my short comments. It is recommended that you get this document. e.g. from the Scottish Green Party and there are 2 other parties in favour. It should help you to put questions to candidates as the majority of people and smaller companies would benefit from not paying the unfair Council and Corporation Taxes at present being levied.

9. Chapters include Context and history, Political and academic interest in LVT, What is land? What is land value taxation? Land value tax and other taxes, Land value tax - making it happen, Land use and ownership, Valuation and use, LVT for Scotland, Comparison with Council Tax, An alternative budget, The full policy proposal, Conclusions and Q&A, References, Appendix.

The question you can ask yourself is why has it been rejected over the years when half the land is owned by only 400 people!

A More Equal and Better Society?

The Answer from the Green Party

The Green movement has long said that the old economic system was unstable and unsustainable, and recent events have confirmed this view.

By placing such an emphasis on GDP and continual growth, previous Governments have lumped together the good and bad aspects of economic activity, and in doing so have neglected to take account of non-material wealth.

Unfortunately, despite all the evidence to show that the old ways aren't working, this is still the model that the other political parties are pushing.

Greens offer an alternative. Rather than prioritising consumerism, Greens believe that economic policy should also take quality of life into account - things such as our health, our relationships, and our sense of community.

In order to ensure a fairer and more equal society, Greens believe that the universal approach to benefits must be defended. A citizen's income - a universal payment sufficient to cover the basic costs of living - would replace means testing and put an end to the benefits trap.

The majority of people work hard in ordinary jobs, but the unrealistic minimum wage means that in-work poverty remains a serious problem, as is the excessive pay and bonus culture amongst some Chief Executives. As well as increasing the minimum wage to the level of a living wage, Greens believe there should be maximum wage ratios in the public sector and, ultimately, throughout the private sector.

Greens would support better parental leave for all parents, protect the interests of older people by investing in housing and providing a Citizens'

Pension at a genuinely liveable level, and would use the benefits system to recognise the role of volunteers and carers in our society.

Financial Services

Over the last few years we have seen the huge problems that are caused by megabanks - those that are "too big to fail", and which combine retail banking and casino-style investment divisions. Greens believe that the immense power wielded by these banks should be curbed.

Instead we should be encouraging and supporting mutual financial institutions such as building societies and co-operatives.

Banks that have been bailed out with public funds should be used for public good - investing in small businesses, low-carbon technologies and ethical trade, rather than supporting the arms industry and dirty projects like tar sands.

Enterprise

A green economy is also a social economy. It will mean investment in universities to provide the skills and knowledge we will need as we make the shift towards a low-carbon, low-waste, localised community.

Current government policy fails to protect independent local businesses, and instead favours large multinationals. In contrast, Greens would place a greater emphasis on local economies and small businesses. Reforming public sector procurement policies to let these companies into the process would be a straightforward way to support smaller businesses and local companies.

International

The Greens are the first political movement born in the age of European political and economic union, and we've always seen EU membership as a positive opportunity to make progress on a host of social and environmental objectives. Europe has improved working conditions for millions of people, helped to control the use of toxic chemicals in industry, and put pressure on all member states to live up to basic standards of human rights and equality.

But the EU is also guilty of far too much economic centralisation, and remains dominated by an unsustainable and market-obsessed economic model. Greens want to see strong self-reliant local and regional economies in Europe, instead of pushing for ever greater centralisation. In a more democratic and accountable Europe, power should be placed in the hands of citizens through a stronger Parliament, and greater use of referendums.

Trident

We believe that the possession of weapons of mass destruction is wrong at any time. But the idea of committing tens of billions of pounds to replace Trident at a time when there are real threats to the funding of public services is particularly repulsive. Greens campaign against Trident both inside Parliament, where we won the first ever clear vote against it at Holyrood, and by participating alongside others in the peaceful direct action which has kept this issue on the political agenda in Scotland over the years.

Arms trade

The UK has a long history of profiteering from the arms trade, and has utterly failed to give any meaning to the phrase "ethical foreign policy". Ending government support for arms fairs, banning the export of offensive weapons and regulating private arms brokers and security consultants would take us in the right direction.

UK foreign policy

By participating the illegal and immoral invasion of Iraq, the UK made the world a more dangerous place and further undermined the institutions which are supposed to bring nations together. The UN Security Council remains dominated by the planet's biggest arms dealers, including the UK and US Governments, and must be reformed to ensure fair representation of all the world's people. The UN itself must have the funding and the authority to mediate in conflicts, which will increasingly occur over access to basic resources as a result of climate change.

Global justice and the eradication of poverty

Instead of relying ever more deadly weapons, we argue that peace and security can only be achieved through global justice. The world will never be safe while we allow the obscenity of poverty to continue, and while economic exploitation and illegal occupations continue.

The growth of ethical and fair trade has shown that many people want an alternative which places human dignity above profit, and which tackles poverty and injustice. It's time to make all trade fair trade, by reforming the global rules and reigning in the power of the multinationals.

Society

Every society has some values which are shared, as well as a rich diversity between people. Sadly, like most developed countries, the voices of those promoting consumerism and greed in Scottish society are currently dominant.

Greens believe the things that really matter in life are good health, good relationships with other people, a safe community and decent homes and local environments. Yet the current economic models don't place value in these things, and government policy has continued to promote short term economic gain and consumption instead.

Our economy has grown richer over recent decades, yet governments of all colours have failed to stop the growth of inequality. A chronically unequal society harms all our interests, and the impact on human happiness is now well understood.

Housing

We believe that local communities also need to have more control over the decisions which affect them, such as housing and development. Community ownership of housing, including through co-operatives and housing associations, can create a real sense of the common good among people. Small community-led organisations can also bring real creativity to challenges like local energy schemes, crime prevention and public health.

Equality

Scotland can be proud of progress that has been made in enhancing equality and protecting diversity. However we still have not succeeded in creating a country where all can participate fully in society regardless of race, gender, disability, age, sexual orientation and religion or belief. Tackling discrimination in society doesn't just benefit the individuals concerned, it also benefits our whole society. We believe equality is an important measure of Scotland's progress.

Democracy

For many people, politics has never been more of a turn-off. Our democratic institutions have brought themselves into disrepute over the misuse of taxpayers' money, and though the Scottish Parliament has been quicker to reform itself than Westminster, there are still far too many politicians who refuse to accept any responsibility.

There are many aspects to the problem - governments which can legislate at a whim without a popular majority, political parties which are in hock to millionaire donors, the undermining of Parliament's authority over Government, and the lack of power many voters feel when presented with three or four brands of the same bland political product.

There are solutions to these problems. By joining the Green Party where you are we can discuss how we can reach these goals.

Go online now!

www.scottishgreens.org.uk

EPILOGUE

I am now 86 years old and I am happy that you have got to the end of the interview! Let me leave you with these last words as I reflect on how lucky I have been to have lived when Homo Sapiens has made such momentous discoveries but also plumbed the depth of despair. We became human when we acquired the remarkable characteristics of language and imagination to create other worlds, powerful gods, dogma and superstition as well as literature, art and music.

This evolutionary trait also created anxieties about death and confusion about meaning, choice and morality which has been used by religious leaders to exercise power over their communities for ill and for good. Fortunately, a new wave of rationalism is sweeping Europe but it seems to me that atheists should now turn to a culture of humanism to replace religion with a positive and proactive guide to comfort and console people caught in our inevitable contradictions, emotions and the dilemmas of our mere existence.

Eric Hobsbawm in his conclusion to classic book: "Age of Extremes If humanity is to have a recognisable future, it cannot be by prolonging the past or the present. If we try to build the third millennium on that basis we shall fail. And the price of that failure, that is to say the alternative to a changed society, is DARKNESS."

A Man I Agreed With

by Norman MacCaig

He knew better than to admire a chair
And say *What does it mean?*
He loved everything that accepted
The unfailing hospitality of his five senses.
He would say *Hello, caterpillar* or
So long, Loch Fewin.

He wanted to know
How they came to be what they are;
But he never insulted them by saying
Caterpillar, Loch Fewin, what do you mean?

In this respect he was like God
Though he was godless - He knew the difference
Between *What does it mean to me?*
And *What does it mean?*

That's why he said, half smiling,
Of course, God, like me,
Is an atheist.

Thanks from Ray

Please do not hesitate to send comments to *newton@raypat.plus.com*